Capital in the Shadows

Nishant Prabhakar

Published by Nishant Prabhakar, 2025.

CAPITAL IN THE SHADOWS

First edition. December 27, 2025.

ISBN: 979-8224772582

Written by Nishant Prabhakar.

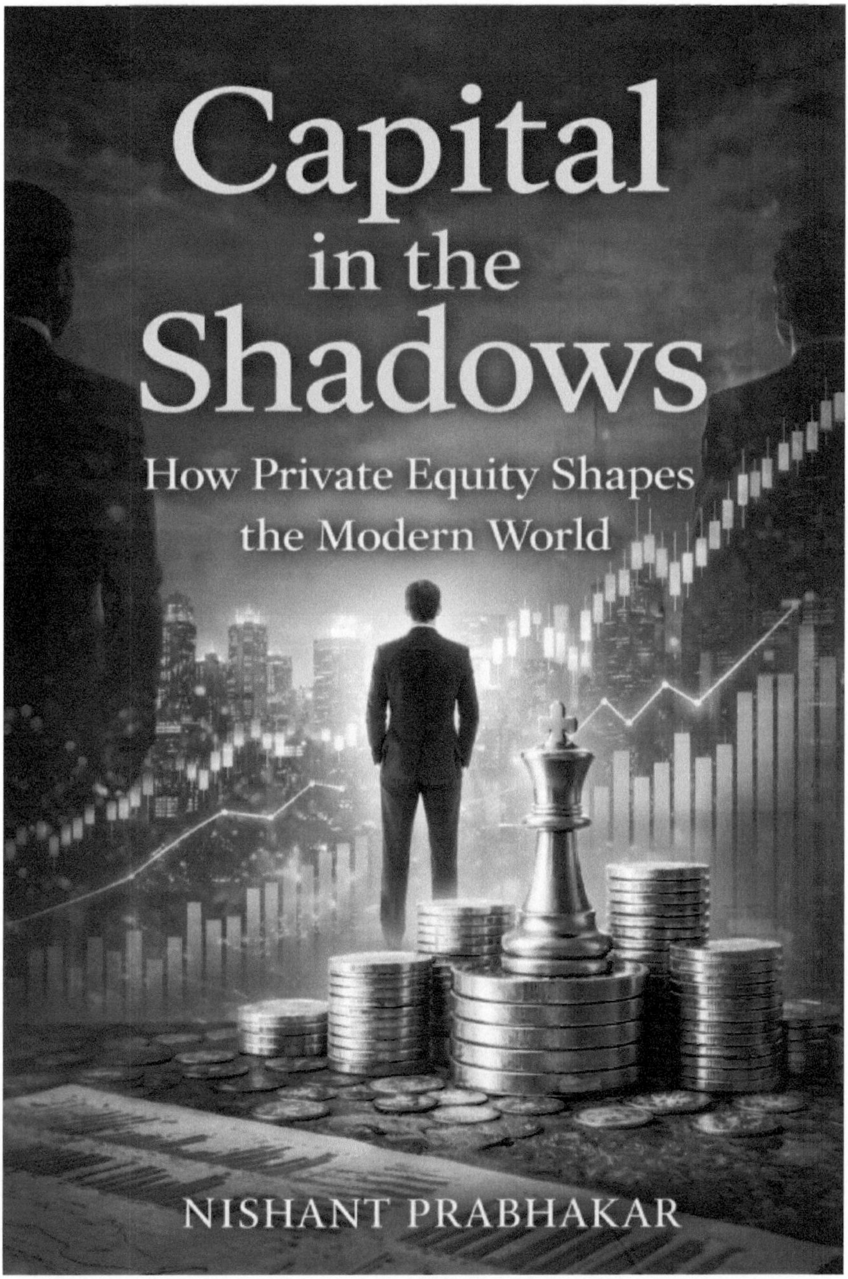
Capital
in the
Shadows
How Private Equity Shapes
the Modern World
NISHANT PRABHAKAR

Table of Contents

Author's Note

This book began as an attempt to answer a deceptively simple question: *What is private equity, really?* Not in the narrow sense of ratios, deal structures, and legal documents, but in the broader sense of a system that shapes companies, careers, and economies. Over time, that question led to another: *How do you explain an industry that is at once intensely technical and deeply human?*

The pages that follow are my attempt to bridge those worlds.

Every chapter in this book has been written from first principles. I have avoided copying, paraphrasing, or leaning on any pre-existing narrative. Instead, I've tried to reconstruct the logic, history, and practice of private equity in my own words, drawing on a wide base of ideas, patterns, and lived realities in global finance and business. Where specific historical events, deal examples, or sector developments are mentioned, they are used for context and illustration, not as anchors for the prose.

This is not an insider's memoir, nor is it a technical manual. It is a hybrid: part history, part textbook, part field guide, and part reflection. My goal has been to make private equity accessible without diluting its complexity; to describe how the industry works in practice, but also to explore what it *means* - for entrepreneurs, employees, investors, and societies.

To keep the narrative honest, I have tried to resist two temptations. The first is the glamorization of private equity as a flawless engine of value creation. The second is the caricature of the industry as a purely extractive force. Reality lies somewhere in between. Private equity can strengthen companies, improve governance, and finance growth that would otherwise not be possible. It can also make mistakes, misjudge risk, and misalign incentives. Both sides deserve to be described clearly.

You will notice a consistent focus on India throughout the book. That is deliberate. India is one of the most fascinating laboratories for private capital anywhere in the world: a young, chaotic, ambitious economy sitting at the intersection of family business traditions, digital disruption, regulatory evolution, and global capital flows. Understanding private equity in India forces us to confront questions of governance, culture, trust, and institutional maturity that are often glossed over in more established markets.

At the same time, this is not "just" a book about India. The frameworks, concepts, and tensions described here apply to private equity in any geography. Capital structure decisions in Mumbai have cousins in New York and London; founder-investor dynamics in Bengaluru echo those in Berlin and São Paulo. The names change, the legal regimes differ, but the underlying challenges are strikingly similar: how to take risk intelligently, how to design incentives, how to govern under uncertainty, and how to build organizations that can survive disruption.

Finally, a word about how to read this book. You do not have to proceed strictly in order. The early chapters provide a historical and conceptual foundation; the middle chapters dive into mechanics and strategy; the later ones explore India, case studies, the LP perspective, and the human side of the industry. Readers new to private equity may wish to start at the beginning and move sequentially. Practitioners may find themselves jumping to chapters on governance, risk, or India-specific themes, then working backwards.

However you choose to approach it, I hope this book helps you see private equity more clearly; not as a mysterious black box, but as a living system with structure, logic, strengths, and flaws. If, by the end, you feel better equipped to ask sharper questions about capital, ownership, and value creation, then this effort will have been worthwhile.

Any errors in judgment, gaps in coverage, or oversimplifications are mine alone. The industry will continue to evolve long after this book is printed; consider this a snapshot in time, written with curiosity, respect for the craft, and a firm belief that good capital, used wisely, can be a powerful force for progress.

Preface

Private equity stands today at a peculiar crossroads. On one hand, it has never been more powerful. Trillions of dollars sit in private funds that own or influence companies in every major sector -healthcare, technology, retail, logistics, manufacturing, energy, infrastructure, and more. On the other hand, it has never been more misunderstood. Outside a relatively small circle of practitioners and institutional investors, private equity is often perceived as opaque, intimidating, or vaguely menacing.

Public discourse tends to oscillate between extremes. In some narratives, private equity is the heroic problem-solver -the capital that rescues distressed companies, the discipline that professionalizes family businesses, the partner that enables innovation. In others, it is the ruthless asset-stripping machine -the force that loads companies with debt, cuts costs mercilessly, and exits before the long-term consequences are felt.

The truth, as usual, is messier.

This book was written in response to three gaps I kept encountering. The first was a conceptual gap: many available explanations either spoke in highly technical language or glossed over essential mechanics. There was room for a work that explained private equity with textbook clarity but narrative warmth -something structured enough for students, detailed enough for practitioners, and readable enough for curious outsiders.

The second gap was geographic. Much of the thinking and writing about private equity remains anchored in American and European experience. While those markets are foundational, they are no longer the only centers of gravity. India, in particular, has emerged as one of the most important arenas for private capital globally. Yet the Indian story has rarely been told in a way that integrates it with the broader evolution of private equity.

The third gap was human. Too many discussions of private equity treat it as a purely numerical game -IRRs, multiples, leverage ratios. In practice, outcomes hinge just as much on people: founders, CEOs, operating partners, junior deal teams, board members, regulators, and employees. Their judgment, incentives, biases, and relationships determine whether capital becomes constructive or destructive.

This book is an attempt to address those gaps.

It begins with history, because any serious understanding of an institution must start with how it came to be. The early chapters situate private equity within centuries of capital pooling, risk sharing, and active ownership. From there, we move into the architecture of modern private equity: the strategies, deal structures, financial concepts, and operating playbooks that define the industry today.

Once the core mechanics are laid out, the narrative shifts to context: how private equity behaves in different geographies, how it evolved in India, how specific case studies illuminate both success and failure. Later chapters examine the perspective of limited partners -the long-term capital that funds private equity -and the human dimension of careers, culture, and decision-making inside firms.

Along the way, certain themes recur. The importance of governance. The fragility of alignment. The tension between financial engineering and real value creation. The difference between owning a company on paper and actually improving it. The necessity of humility in an industry that deals with uncertainty as its daily raw material.

This is not a promotional document. It does not assume that private equity is always the right answer. There are deals that should never be done, companies that should never be leveraged, and sectors where private capital can do more harm than good if misapplied. But it is also true that in many situations -especially in markets undertaking structural change -private equity can be a uniquely effective tool for building resilient, forward-looking businesses.

If you are an aspiring professional, I hope the book demystifies the industry and gives you a framework for deciding whether this is the right path for you. If you are an entrepreneur or business leader, I hope it helps you understand what a private equity partnership can offer -and what it cannot. If you are an investor, policymaker, or observer, I hope it sharpens your view of how private capital fits into the broader fabric of economic development.

Above all, I hope it convinces you of one simple idea: private equity is not just about buying and selling companies. At its best, it is about taking responsibility for them.

Acknowledgements

No book of this scope is truly written alone. Even when the actual writing happens in solitude, the ideas that shape it are forged in conversation, observation, and quiet indebtedness to many people and institutions.

I owe my deepest gratitude to the entrepreneurs and executives who, over the years, have shared candid stories about building, scaling, and sometimes struggling with their companies under private ownership. Their openness about both successes and disappointments has been invaluable. The texture of this book - especially in the chapters on governance, value creation, and the human side of private equity -owes much to insights generously offered in conference rooms, board meetings, and late-night discussions.

I am equally grateful to investors across the spectrum - from early-stage venture partners to large-cap buyout professionals and limited partners at sovereign funds, pensions, and endowments. Conversations with them helped sharpen my understanding of how capital allocators think about risk, alignment, and long-term performance. Many of the frameworks embedded in this book were stress-tested against their questions and critiques, even if they will not recognize their fingerprints directly on the page.

Special thanks are due to those who offered intellectual companionship outside.

CHAPTER 1 - THE BIRTH OF PRIVATE EQUITY

Private equity, as we understand it today, is a sophisticated global system of capital allocation that influences industries, shapes companies, and generates extraordinary wealth. Yet its origins stretch back far beyond the modern financial era. Its foundations lie in the earliest attempts by human societies to pool capital, share risk, and back individuals with ambition and ideas. This chapter traces the evolutionary arc of private equity - from medieval merchant partnerships to industrial-age financiers, from the first pooled investment vehicles to the institutions that laid the blueprint for modern venture capital and buyouts.

The origins of private equity are not just financial; they are deeply tied to human ingenuity, technological progress, and the changing structures of commerce. The story is one of continuity and reinvention, showing that the fundamental principles of private equity - long-term risk taking, active ownership, governance, and value creation - have been present for centuries, even as the tools and terminology evolved.

1. Early Capital Pools: Merchant Guilds and Proto-Private Equity

Long before modern banks, regulators, or financial markets, commerce was driven by networks of merchants who formed early risk-sharing partnerships. Medieval Italian families such as the Medicis and the Fuggers were among the earliest practitioners of what could be considered proto-private equity. They deployed capital into trade expeditions, mining ventures, and artisanal industries, taking on risks that traditional lenders avoided.

These partnerships were small by modern standards, but they contained the core components of private equity. The merchant-financiers provided capital; the entrepreneurs provided labor and operational capability; and both parties participated in profits and losses. The financiers actively monitored the ventures, sometimes sending trusted agents to oversee operations. Early agreements defined terms for profit distribution, governance, and conflict resolution, establishing a structure that resembles today's limited partnership model.

Capital scarcity made these arrangements vital. Without publicly traded corporations or standardized banking systems, ambitious projects - such as opening new trade routes, building ships, or developing early manufacturing processes - required investors willing to embrace uncertainty. The merchant partnership model served as the institutional backbone of international trade and economic expansion during this era.

Even in this embryonic stage, private equity reflected a simple truth: bold ideas require bold capital. The merchants who financed exploration, mining, and early manufacturing were not only traders; they were the venture capitalists and buyout specialists of their time.

2. The Age of Exploration: Syndicated Risk and Venture-Style Investing

The expansion of global trade during the 15th to 17th centuries introduced a new form of investment: the expedition syndicate. Funding transoceanic voyages demanded enormous capital and carried unpredictable risks - shipwrecks, piracy, navigation challenges, and geopolitical conflict. Few individuals could shoulder these risks alone, so wealthy backers pooled funds to finance expeditions led by navigators and explorers.

These syndicates exhibited many features recognizable in modern venture capital. Investors made long-term bets on high-risk, high-reward ventures. They backed individuals - explorers, merchants, navigators - whose reputations and expertise inspired confidence. Returns were not linear; most voyages yielded little, but a few produced enormous profits from spices, commodities, or territorial claims.

The payoff structure resembled the power-law distribution that defines venture capital today: many losses or modest returns, punctuated by transformative winners. Success required not only capital, but a deep tolerance for uncertainty and the vision to see opportunity in uncharted territory.

Over time, these expedition ventures laid the groundwork for more institutionalized capital pools. The need for sustained funding and professional management spurred financial innovations that would reshape global commerce.

---

3. Joint-Stock Companies: The First Institutional Private Market

The creation of the joint-stock company in the 17th century - most famously the Dutch East India Company (VOC) and the British East India Company - represents a pivotal moment in the evolution of private equity. For the first time, investors could purchase fractional shares in a commercial enterprise, spreading risk among many participants while enabling ventures of unprecedented scale.

The earliest joint-stock companies operated more like private capital pools than modern public corporations. Shares were not freely traded on open exchanges; ownership transfers were limited and often arranged privately. Managers exercised broad discretion, acting as active stewards of investor capital. The companies deployed substantial leverage, negotiated trade monopolies, managed logistics networks, and oversaw large staffs of administrators and laborers.

The VOC, in particular, was revolutionary. It managed overseas territories, operated a naval fleet, funded military campaigns, and generated extraordinary profits. Investors enjoyed returns that would impress even today's most aggressive private equity funds. The company's governance structure - featuring elected directors, performance reporting, and shareholder rights - set precedents that persist in corporate finance.

Joint-stock companies institutionalized two essential principles: the separation of ownership and management, and the pooling of large capital bases for long-term, risky ventures. These innovations brought scale to private investment and laid the foundation for modern financial markets.

---

4. Industrialization and the Rise of Financial Intermediaries

The industrial revolution of the 18th and 19th centuries ushered in an era of massive capital requirements. Factories, railroads, mining operations, steel plants, and mechanized textile mills required long-term financing that exceeded the capacity of traditional local lenders. Entrepreneurs needed investors who not only supplied capital but also understood complex operational and technological challenges.

This environment gave rise to sophisticated financiers who played roles remarkably similar to modern private equity sponsors. In the United States, J.P. Morgan became synonymous with industrial restructuring. Morgan's interventions in the railroad industry - which suffered from overbuilding, mismanagement, and financial distress - foreshadowed the buyout model. He imposed governance reforms, installed competent management, consolidated fragmented networks, and renegotiated debt structures.

In effect, Morgan conducted early leveraged buyouts, acquiring control of distressed railroads and leading large-scale turnarounds. His work demonstrated that financial discipline combined with operational restructuring could salvage struggling enterprises and generate outsized returns. European financiers like the Rothschilds took similar approaches in mining, railways, and public infrastructure.

Industrialization also spurred the rise of investment partnerships and private credit arrangements. Wealthy industrialists and merchant families invested in ventures through informal but structured agreements that formalized responsibilities, profit sharing, and oversight. These arrangements were precursors to the limited partnerships that dominate modern private equity.

By the turn of the 20th century, the essential toolkit of private equity - governance intervention, financial restructuring, active ownership, and strategic oversight - was firmly in place, even if the terminology had not yet emerged.

5. Post-War Reconstruction and the First Modern Venture Funds

World War II devastated Europe's industrial base, disrupted global trade, and exhausted national treasuries. In the aftermath, entrepreneurs needed capital to rebuild factories, revive supply chains, and pursue innovation. Yet traditional lenders were unwilling to extend credit to unproven ventures in a fragile economic environment.

This mismatch between capital needs and risk tolerance created a structural opportunity for private investors. The most important innovation of this era was the founding of American Research and Development Corporation (ARDC) in 1946. Led by MIT president Karl Compton and financier Ralph Flanders, ARDC sought to deploy institutional capital into high-risk, high-growth companies - a radically new concept.

ARDC pioneered the modern venture capital model. It raised capital from universities, insurance companies, and endowments, assembled a professional investment team, and evaluated early-stage companies on the basis of technology, talent, and long-term potential. Its most famous investment - a $70,000 stake in Digital Equipment Corporation (DEC) - grew into a value exceeding $350 million upon IPO, validating the power of patient, high-risk equity investing.

ARDC was the first demonstration that professionalized private investing could generate returns competitive with, or superior to, public markets. It inspired the founding of later venture firms in Silicon Valley and laid the intellectual foundations for private equity's expansion. The idea that institutions could - and should - allocate part of their portfolios to long-term private investments reshaped global capital allocation.

6. The Emergence of the Buyout Era

While venture capital focused on startup growth, another branch of private equity emerged: the control buyout. Throughout the 1960s and 1970s, American corporations grew rapidly and diversified into conglomerates. Many divisions were poorly managed or strategically misaligned, creating opportunities for investors willing to acquire and restructure them.

Jerome Kohlberg, Henry Kravis, and George Roberts recognized this opportunity. Their work at Bear Stearns and later their founding of KKR in 1976 formalized the leveraged buyout (LBO) as a distinct strategy. By using debt to acquire companies and then applying operational and financial discipline, KKR demonstrated that undervalued or underperforming businesses could be transformed into profitable enterprises.

The LBO model depended on several innovations: the use of leverage to enhance returns, the acquisition of majority control to enable governance changes, and the application of rigorous performance metrics. Early buyouts were often small or mid-sized, but as the model proved successful, deal sizes expanded dramatically.

The milestone moment came with the RJR Nabisco buyout in 1989 - a $31 billion acquisition chronicled in *Barbarians at the Gate*. The deal symbolized both the ambition and excess of the buyout boom. While controversial, it cemented the LBO as a permanent part of global finance and demonstrated that private firms could orchestrate transactions on a scale once reserved for public markets.

7. Institutional Capital and the Codification of Private Equity

By the 1990s, private equity had evolved from a niche strategy into an institutional asset class. Pension funds, endowments, and sovereign wealth funds recognized the superior long-term returns generated by top-tier private equity firms. This influx of capital fuelled the growth of buyout funds, venture capital firms, and new hybrid strategies.

The limited partnership (LP–GP) structure became the industry standard. General partners raised capital in fixed-life funds, invested across cycles, and returned capital and profits to limited partners. This structure created alignment of interests, disciplined investment pacing, and performance incentives that contributed to the industry's credibility and success.

At the same time, globalization expanded the opportunity set. European and Asian markets opened to private investment, cross-border deals became common, and multinational corporations began divesting non-core units, creating fertile ground for carve-outs and strategic acquisitions. Private equity was no longer just an American phenomenon; it became a global force.

Moreover, the technology boom of the late 1990s and the subsequent dot-com crash further legitimized private equity strategies. Venture capital demonstrated its power to create new industries, while buyout firms proved resilient in restructuring distressed companies. The contrasting experiences highlighted the complementary nature of different private equity strategies within the broader ecosystem.

8. Private Equity's Modern Form: Multi-Strategy Platforms and Global Powerhouses

The early 21st century saw the emergence of large, diversified private equity firms. Firms such as Blackstone, KKR, Carlyle, TPG, and Apollo expanded across asset classes and geographies. They raised capital in private credit, real estate, infrastructure, hedge funds, and specialized sector strategies. These multi-strategy platforms became global asset managers rather than traditional buyout firms.

Their growth transformed private equity into a central pillar of global capital markets. PE-owned companies became major employers, and PE-backed transactions reshaped industries ranging from healthcare and logistics to technology and retail. The influence of private equity - once limited to corporate finance - extended into public policy, labor markets, and economic development.

By the 2020s, private equity had become a defining force of modern capitalism. Its ability to deploy capital quickly, influence strategic direction, and generate operational improvements made it indispensable in both mature and emerging markets.

Conclusion: The Continuity of Capital and the Arc of Private Equity

From medieval merchants to global asset managers, the evolution of private equity reflects enduring principles that transcend time: the willingness to take risk, the need to actively steward capital, and the belief that transformative ideas deserve patient, engaged investors.

Although the terminology changed, the underlying impulses remained constant. Early voyagers seeking financiers, industrial magnates restructuring factories, and modern private equity sponsors improving companies all engaged in the same fundamental pursuit: deploying capital to unlock potential.

Private equity's journey from informal merchant guilds to multi-trillion-dollar platforms illustrates how financial innovation evolves continuously, shaped by economic conditions, technological progress, and human ambition. Its history provides insight into its present - and offers clues about the future trajectory of global capitalism.

CHAPTER 2 - GLOBAL PRIVATE EQUITY TODAY

Private equity has matured into one of the most important and influential systems of capital allocation in the modern world. It is no longer a peripheral investment strategy or a niche alternative asset class; rather, it is a global architecture that helps determine how companies evolve, how industries consolidate, and how capital flows across markets. What began in the United States has expanded into a geographically diverse and strategically sophisticated ecosystem that now shapes the trajectory of entire national economies.

The story of global private equity is the story of how financial innovation, institutional demand, technological progress, and entrepreneurial ambition converged to create a force that influences everything from healthcare and retail to logistics, software, infrastructure, and energy transition. Today, private equity is vast, complex, and deeply interconnected. Understanding its contours requires examining both the breadth of its expansion and the depth of its evolving strategies.

---

1. The Scale and Architecture of Modern Private Equity

The modern private equity industry is enormous in size. While early practitioners managed modest pools of capital, the industry now oversees trillions of dollars across multiple strategies. This growth reflects a profound shift in the global investment landscape, driven by the shortcomings of public markets, the hunger for long-term returns among institutional investors, and the increasing belief that private ownership offers a superior environment for operational transformation.

Private equity today is not a monolithic activity but a constellation of strategies: buyouts, venture capital, growth equity, private credit, infrastructure, real estate, special situations, and secondaries, among others. Large firms operate across all of these verticals, forming multi-strategy platforms that allow them to influence deals at every stage of the corporate lifecycle. Capital is raised from a broad set of limited partners - pension funds, sovereign wealth funds, endowments, foundations, insurance companies, and an increasing number of family offices and ultra-high-net-worth platforms.

This scale has made private equity a central pillar of modern finance. PE-backed companies now employ millions of people, form a substantial share of national corporate sectors, and often outperform comparable public market peers in productivity, margins, and growth. The magnitude of this influence is only possible because private equity has become global.

2. The United States: The Epicenter of Private Equity

The United States remains the gravitational center of the global private equity industry. This is not merely a consequence of early leadership but the result of structural advantages that continue to attract capital and deal flow. The U.S. boasts deep and liquid credit markets, allowing firms to structure sophisticated financing packages for buyouts. Its entrepreneurial culture fosters a constant pipeline of growth-stage and late-stage companies seeking capital. And its regulatory environment - although complex - provides predictability, investor protection, and strong enforcement of contracts.

The American pension system, particularly public pension funds and university endowments, played a crucial role in scaling private equity. Endowments such as Yale and Harvard embraced alternatives earlier than most institutional pools, recognizing the value of long-duration, illiquid investments. Their decades of success created a template that countless other LPs followed.

In addition, the corporate structure of the U.S. - with frequent divestitures, corporate carve-outs, and professional management teams - provides a fertile environment for buyouts. Many of the most iconic private equity deals in history originated in the U.S., reinforcing its role as both a proving ground and an exporter of best practices to the rest of the world.

---

3. Europe: A Sophisticated but Complex Market

Europe's private equity landscape is one of sophistication layered over complexity. Unlike the United States, Europe is not a single market but a collection of distinct regulatory systems, languages, business cultures, and economic environments. This fragmentation presents challenges, but it also creates opportunities that skilled investors eagerly pursue.

European private equity evolved differently from its American counterpart. Whereas the U.S. market grew through buyouts of widely held corporations and divestitures, much of Europe's opportunity set lies in family-owned businesses. Many European families prefer to remain involved, resulting in creative ownership structures and minority control strategies. Private equity firms in Europe must therefore balance financial engineering with diplomacy, succession planning, and cultural sensitivity.

In addition, Europe has been fertile ground for sector specialization. Nordic firms often emphasize sustainability-oriented investments and industrial technology. UK-based firms excel in consumer brands and healthcare. France and Germany present opportunities in manufacturing, luxury, and industrial automation.

This regional diversity has produced some of the world's most respected global funds - firms like EQT, CVC, Ardian, Cinven, Apax Partners, and Permira - which have expanded far beyond their home markets and now execute deals across continents.

4. China: A Rapid Rise Followed by Recalibration

China's ascent in private capital markets during the early 21st century was nothing short of spectacular. Fuelled by massive urbanization, the proliferation of smartphones, and a vibrant tech ecosystem, China became one of the world's most dynamic hubs for venture capital and growth equity. Investments in companies like Alibaba, Tencent, JD.com, Meituan, Didi, and ByteDance produced enormous returns, attracting global attention and unprecedented capital inflows.

However, the landscape has changed markedly in recent years. Regulatory tightening, government scrutiny of large technology platforms, restrictions on overseas IPOs, and geopolitical tensions have forced both domestic and foreign investors to reassess their strategies. The result is not a collapse but a recalibration.

China remains critical to global private equity due to its scale, innovation capacity, and domestic capital formation. Yet the era of unconstrained global participation has given way to a new phase where local currency funds, state-linked investors, and domestically focused strategies dominate. The trajectory of China's private equity market now aligns more closely with national priorities, industrial policy, and internal capital circulation.

5. India: The World's Most Promising Private Equity Frontier

India stands out as one of the most compelling long-term private equity opportunities globally. With its youthful demographics, rapidly expanding middle class, high-velocity digital adoption, and increasingly formalized economy, India presents a rare combination of scale, growth, and institutional development.

The transformation began after the 1991 economic liberalization, which opened the economy to foreign investment and unleashed a wave of entrepreneurship. The rise of the IT and outsourcing sectors attracted global capital and established credibility. Over time, the financial ecosystem deepened: domestic private equity funds emerged, regulatory frameworks matured, capital markets strengthened, and the Indian IPO market became one of the most vibrant in Asia.

Yet India's private equity landscape has its own unique character. Family-owned enterprises dominate the corporate sector, meaning buyouts are less common and minority growth investments are more prevalent. Deal-making often hinges on founder relations, governance negotiations, and alignment on long-term vision. Nevertheless, global firms such as Blackstone, KKR, TPG, and Warburg Pincus - together with homegrown giants like ChrysCapital, True North, Multiples, Premji Invest, and Matrix - have established deep footprints.

India's digital economy represents the newest wave of opportunity. Cheap mobile data, widespread fintech adoption, and government infrastructure platforms have created fertile ground for venture capital and late-stage growth investments. As the country aims to transition to a multi-trillion-dollar economy, private equity is set to play a pivotal role in that evolution.

---

6. Southeast Asia, the Middle East, and Africa: The Emerging Frontiers

Beyond the established markets in the U.S., Europe, China, and India, private equity is expanding into frontier regions that offer demographic tailwinds and structural growth drivers.

Southeast Asia, led by Indonesia, Vietnam, the Philippines, and Malaysia, is characterized by young populations, rising incomes, and accelerating digital adoption. Singapore serves as the region's financial and operational hub, enabling regional expansion even in fragmented regulatory environments.

The Middle East has become a major provider of global private capital, not merely an allocator. Sovereign wealth funds such as ADIA, Mubadala, PIF, and QIA now invest directly in large deals worldwide, sometimes alongside global private equity firms and sometimes independently. Their influence shapes deal flow, capital availability, and competitive dynamics globally.

Africa, though still an early-stage private equity market, presents long-term potential. Urbanization, rising consumption, infrastructure needs, and a growing entrepreneurial ecosystem provide opportunities across sectors such as fintech, agriculture, telecom infrastructure, and healthcare. Investments require patience and deep local insight, but the continent's trajectory suggests increasing relevance in global private capital flows.

7. The Shift from Financial Engineering to Operational Mastery

One of the most profound transformations in global private equity has been the evolution from reliance on leverage to an emphasis on operational value creation. While debt remains an important lever, the primary source of alpha now lies in improving the underlying business.

Operating partners - once a novelty - are now integral to most top-tier private equity firms. These individuals bring decades of industry experience and work closely with management teams to redesign processes, upgrade technology systems, restructure pricing models, expand into new markets, and strengthen leadership teams. Playbooks for operational transformation have become increasingly sophisticated and data-driven.

This shift also reflects the changing expectations of limited partners, who want assurance that returns are not simply the product of financial arbitrage. As competition intensifies, firms differentiate themselves through execution, not just capital. Operational mastery has become the cornerstone of sustainable performance and a key pillar of modern private equity strategy.

8. The Rise of Multi-Strategy Private Equity Firms

In parallel with operational sophistication, private equity firms have evolved into multi-strategy platforms. Instead of limiting themselves to traditional buyouts, firms now operate across private credit, real estate, infrastructure, venture capital, insurance solutions, and secondary markets.

This diversification creates stability in fundraising, improves access to deals, and broadens the firm's ability to structure complex transactions. For example, a modern private equity platform might finance a deal's debt component through its credit arm, acquire the company through its buyout fund, own its property assets through its real estate division, and ultimately sell the investment to its secondaries platform. This creates a tightly integrated ecosystem where capital flows efficiently and strategically.

Multi-strategy firms enjoy significant competitive advantages. Their size and brand recognition attract top management teams, their relationships grant access to proprietary deal flow, and their broad product suites create enduring loyalty among LPs. This model - pioneered by firms such as Blackstone, KKR, Apollo, Carlyle, and EQT - is now the dominant architecture of global private equity.

9. Private Credit: A Parallel Revolution Reshaping Corporate Finance

The global financial crisis of 2008 fundamentally reshaped credit markets. As banks retreated from leveraged lending due to regulatory pressure and higher capital requirements, private credit funds stepped in to fill the void. What began as a niche form of lending has grown into a massive asset class that now rivals traditional banking channels in the financing of mid-market and large-cap companies.

Private lenders offer speed, flexibility, and certainty of execution that banks struggle to match. They can structure bespoke financing packages, move quickly in competitive auctions, and support acquisitions that require nuanced capital structures. As a result, many private equity deals today are financed primarily through private credit rather than syndicated bank loans.

This shift has deep strategic implications. Private equity firms increasingly integrate credit capabilities into their platforms, creating symbiotic relationships between buyout and lending strategies. It also means that private markets now influence corporate capital structures in ways once reserved for banks, altering the balance of power in global finance.

---

10. Technology's Expanding Role in Private Equity

Technology has become one of the most important levers in the modern private equity toolkit. From deal sourcing and due diligence to portfolio management and value creation, data analytics and digital tools now play a central role in shaping firm strategy.

Artificial intelligence and machine learning allow firms to identify early signals of business momentum - changes in hiring trends, online customer sentiment, app downloads, web traffic, and operational bottlenecks. These tools enable investors to spot opportunities long before they appear on broker radars.

Digital transformation is equally important in portfolio management. Companies owned by private equity increasingly use cloud-based financial systems, predictive analytics for operations, and digital twins to model future scenarios. PE firms no longer rely solely on consultants for insight; they build in-house expertise that deploys across multiple portfolio companies, allowing for faster and more informed decision-making.

The result is a more competitive marketplace where access to data, technology, and analytical capability becomes a critical differentiator - on par with capital itself.

---

11. The Changing Dynamic Between Limited Partners and Private Equity Firms

The relationship between limited partners and private equity firms has evolved significantly. LPs are no longer passive capital providers; they are sophisticated partners who negotiate hard on fees, demand co-investment rights, and increasingly operate direct investment programs.

Sovereign wealth funds, in particular, have emerged as influential players. Entities such as ADIA, Mubadala, GIC, Temasek, and PIF deploy vast sums globally, sometimes partnering with private equity firms and sometimes competing with them. Large pension funds - notably in Canada and the Netherlands - have also built direct investment arms capable of underwriting large deals internally.

This new dynamic introduces both opportunity and complexity. PE firms gain access to larger pools of capital and can structure larger transactions, but they must also navigate a more demanding LP base that expects transparency and alignment.

12. Why Companies Prefer Private Markets

The shift from public to private markets is one of the defining investment trends of the last two decades. The number of public companies in the United States has nearly halved since the late 1990s, while the number of private equity-backed companies has surged.

Public markets impose quarterly reporting pressures, expose companies to activist shareholders, and demand transparency that can be counterproductive during complex restructuring or transformation efforts. Private markets offer the opposite: the freedom to experiment, reorganize, and pursue long-term strategies without the glare of public scrutiny.

As a result, many high-growth technology companies now prefer to remain private much longer than in prior decades. Late-stage rounds from private equity firms and sovereign wealth funds increasingly function as "private IPOs," providing substantial capital without the burdens of listing. This trend has contributed to the sustained growth of the private capital ecosystem.

13. Specialization as the New Edge

As private equity has matured, specialization has become a crucial competitive advantage. Broad strategies are no longer sufficient in a crowded marketplace where capital is abundant and information is widely available. Instead, firms win by focusing deeply on particular sectors or sub-sectors where they can develop proprietary knowledge, relationships, and operational insights.

Some firms excel in enterprise software, others in business services, healthcare, logistics, or consumer brands. The rise of specialist funds reflects a broader reality: value creation now depends more on industry understanding than on leverage or financial engineering. PE firms must understand the nuances of industry cycles, technology disruption, regulatory frameworks, and customer behavior to outperform over the long run.

---

14. The Emerging Future of Global Private Equity

Looking forward, several trends will shape the next era of private equity. India and Southeast Asia are poised to become major growth engines for the industry, thanks to their demographic dividends, digital transformation, and ongoing economic formalization. Energy transition and climate investing represent another major frontier, requiring massive capital deployment into renewable energy, electric mobility, battery storage, and green infrastructure.

The secondaries market, once a mechanism for liquidity, has grown into a structural part of private markets - enabling continuation funds, GP-led restructurings, and multi-asset rollovers. This trend will accelerate as funds mature and companies remain private longer.

Finally, technology will continue to redefine how private equity operates. AI-driven sourcing, analytics-powered value creation, and automated due diligence will become mainstream. Firms with superior technological and analytical capabilities will gain significant competitive advantages.

Conclusion: Private Equity as a Global Engine of Transformation

Private equity today operates at the intersection of finance, strategy, and entrepreneurship. It is no longer merely a mechanism for acquiring companies; it is a system for reshaping them. Its global reach, operational sophistication, and capacity for long-term value creation have made it a central force in the world economy.

The industry's evolution from niche financier to global architect of corporate transformation reflects its adaptability and resilience. As private equity continues to expand across markets, sectors, and strategies, its influence will only deepen - setting the stage for the next chapter in the history of modern capitalism and the future of global investment.

CHAPTER 3 - DEVELOPMENT OF PRIVATE EQUITY IN INDIA

Private equity in India is a relatively young phenomenon when viewed against the centuries-long evolution of global private capital. Yet in less than three decades, India has become one of the most active, dynamic, and promising private equity markets in the world. The country's rise reflects the interplay of economic liberalization, demographic momentum, capital market reforms, entrepreneurial energy, digital transformation, and institutional maturity.

The Indian private equity ecosystem did not emerge fully formed. It evolved through phases - from early foreign portfolio investors cautiously deploying capital in the 1990s, to the growth equity boom of the 2000s, to the startup revolution of the 2010s, and into the current era of large-scale buyouts, specialized sector strategies, domestic institutional participation, and sophisticated governance.

This chapter describes how private equity took root in India, the distinctive characteristics of the market, the role that global and domestic investors played in shaping modern Indian capitalism, and the unique opportunities and constraints that define the landscape today.

---

1. The Pre-Liberalization Era: Foundations Without a Market

Before 1991, India had no meaningful private equity market. The economy was governed by license-based industrial policies, foreign investment restrictions, high tariff barriers, and limited entrepreneurship outside a few family-owned conglomerates. Capital formation came primarily from public sector banks, government institutions, and retained corporate earnings.

The concept of outside investors taking minority stakes in private businesses was culturally unfamiliar and institutionally unsupported. Corporate governance norms were undeveloped, disclosure requirements were minimal, and the regulatory architecture was fragmented. Entrepreneurship existed, but its scale was constrained by regulation, bureaucracy, and lack of risk capital.

However, even in this restrictive environment, certain seeds for future private equity activity were planted. The rise of Indian multinationals like the Tatas, Birlas, and Bajaj demonstrated the potential for long-term industrial growth. Public financial institutions such as IDBI and ICICI engaged in quasi-private-equity-style project financing. A nascent IT industry emerged in Bangalore and Hyderabad. These early developments indicated that with the right policy environment, India could become fertile ground for private capital.

2. The 1991 Reforms: Opening the Doors to Private Investment

India's economic liberalization in 1991 was a watershed moment. Facing a balance-of-payments crisis, the government undertook sweeping reforms: reducing import tariffs, deregulating industries, allowing foreign investment, dismantling licensing requirements, and reforming capital markets.

These reforms fundamentally changed the country's economic direction. For the first time, foreign institutional investors (FIIs) and venture capital firms could deploy capital into Indian companies. The earliest private equity investments came from global development finance institutions such as IFC, CDC, and ADB, which supported infrastructure, manufacturing, and early technology ventures.

Domestic financial institutions also began experimenting with quasi-venture capital programs. However, the ecosystem remained thin. Deal flow was limited to a small number of emerging tech companies, export-focused manufacturers, and consumer businesses run by progressive family entrepreneurs. Private equity was still a new and somewhat foreign idea - viewed with curiosity, caution, and occasional suspicion.

Nevertheless, the reforms created an irreversible momentum. As India opened up, entrepreneurs emerged who were global in outlook, ambitious in scale, and receptive to outside capital. This early period laid the groundwork for the explosive growth that would follow.

3. The Early 2000s: The Formation of India's First PE Wave

Between 2000 and 2008, private equity in India entered its first real period of expansion. The global technology boom increased investor interest in India's IT and IT-enabled services (ITES) industries. Companies such as Infosys, Wipro, TCS, Satyam, and Cognizant demonstrated that Indian firms could compete globally, attract global investors, and generate significant shareholder returns.

Several trends converged to fuel the industry's rise.

The first was India's demographic advantage - a young workforce entering the global labor market just as outsourcing demand surged worldwide. The second was the formalization of India's capital markets through SEBI reforms, improved corporate disclosure requirements, and stronger governance norms. The third was the growing recognition by global private equity giants - Warburg Pincus, KKR, Blackstone, Carlyle, TPG - that India represented an underserved high-growth market.

Warburg Pincus' landmark $292 million investment in Bharti Airtel in 2000 became one of the most successful private equity deals in global history. It validated the potential for long-term minority investing in

India and demonstrated that patient capital could generate transformational returns.

During this period, domestic firms also began to emerge. ChrysCapital, ICICI Venture, IDFC Private Equity, and Kotak Private Equity established themselves as early Indian private equity pioneers. Their familiarity with local business culture, regulatory complexities, and founder psychology gave them an advantage over global firms still learning the Indian market.

This early phase was characterized by strong returns, expanding deal flow, and growing institutional confidence in India. It set the stage for the boom that would follow.

4. The Growth Equity Boom (2005–2010): Capital Meets Consumption

Between 2005 and 2010, private equity investment in India surged dramatically. This period saw capital inflows into a wide range of sectors - telecom, financial services, banking, real estate, infrastructure, and consumer goods. India's GDP growth consistently exceeded 8%, creating an optimistic environment for both entrepreneurs and investors.

The growth equity model - minority investments in rapidly expanding businesses - became the dominant strategy in India. This approach fit the Indian context for several reasons. Most mid-sized Indian companies were family-run and reluctant to give up control. Banks were conservative lenders, limiting debt-financed buyouts. The entrepreneurial ecosystem was expanding, generating a steady supply of companies seeking capital for expansion.

Real estate and infrastructure saw exaggerated inflows during this period, with some investments later proving unsustainable. But the boom also created long-term winners, particularly in financial services. Private equity played a critical role in scaling non-bank financial companies (NBFCs), housing finance firms, and microfinance institutions, many of which later became public companies.

The government's emphasis on infrastructure investment also attracted private capital. However, regulatory complexity and execution risks made this an uneven sector for returns. Nonetheless, the 2005–2010 period represented a turning point: India was no longer a frontier market for private equity - it was a core allocation for global investors.

5. The Post-Global Financial Crisis Reset (2010–2015)

The global financial crisis of 2008–09 had a delayed but significant impact on India. Returns fell, IPO markets froze, and several over-leveraged companies entered distress. Private equity firms struggled with exits, leading to more cautious investment strategies.

However, this period was also one of institutional strengthening. PE firms established deeper on-the-ground teams, developed sector expertise, and built better relationships with promoters. Domestic investors became more sophisticated, and regulatory oversight improved.

A pivotal shift occurred in investor expectations. The earlier era of rapid multiple expansion gave way to a focus on operational value creation, governance improvement, and disciplined underwriting. Investors now paid close attention to revenue quality, cash flows, compliance, and alignment with founders.

This period also saw the emergence of specialized funds - focused on healthcare, education, consumer brands, and financial services. India's private equity ecosystem matured significantly during these years, creating a foundation for the digital revolution to come.

6. The Startup & Venture Capital Revolution (2015–2020)

India's private equity landscape transformed again in the mid-2010s with the rise of the startup economy. Fuelled by cheap smartphones, affordable data, and the launch of digital infrastructure like Aadhaar and UPI, India became one of the fastest-growing technology ecosystems in the world.

Global venture capital funds - Sequoia, Accel, Tiger Global, SoftBank, Lightspeed, Matrix, Elevation - poured billions into Indian startups. Domestic funds emerged to complement them. Categories like fintech, e-commerce, mobility, SaaS, D2C brands, edtech, and healthtech saw explosive growth.

Startups such as Flipkart, Paytm, Byju's, OYO, Swiggy, Zomato, Ola, PhonePe, Pine Labs, Razorpay, Freshworks, and Nykaa reshaped India's entrepreneurial narrative. Private equity firms also entered late-stage venture deals, enabling startups to scale aggressively.

This revolution created new exit pathways. India saw a wave of tech IPOs, cross-border M&A, and secondary transactions, proving that India's startup ecosystem could generate liquidity for investors.

The 2015–2020 period marked India's arrival as a global innovation hub - and private capital played a central role in funding its rise.

7. The Rise of Large-Scale Buyouts (2017–Present)

Buyouts were historically rare in India due to promoter reluctance, conservative lending, and cultural preference for family control. But over the last decade, large-scale buyouts have become increasingly common.

Several factors drove this shift: generational transitions in family businesses, rising corporate debt, succession challenges, governance issues, and growing trust in global PE firms. Private equity sponsors demonstrated the ability to professionalize management, scale businesses, and improve governance.

Blackstone became India's largest buyout firm, executing marquee deals in IT services, real estate, manufacturing, and consumer sectors. KKR, Advent, Bain Capital, Carlyle, TPG, and Baring Asia also completed significant buyouts across healthcare, financial services, consumer brands, and industrials.

Domestic banks and NBFCs began supporting leveraged transactions selectively, while private credit funds provided flexible capital structures. As a result, buyouts have become a mainstream strategy, particularly in mid-market and upper-mid-market segments.

8. Domestic LPs and the Emergence of Indian Private Capital

For many years, India's private equity ecosystem relied heavily on foreign capital. But domestic investors - family offices, insurance companies, corporate treasuries, and sovereign institutions - are now playing a larger role.

Indian family offices have begun allocating to private equity both directly and through funds. Sovereign institutions like NIIF have become important participants, especially in infrastructure and strategic sectors. Domestic pension reform and the growth of AIFs (Alternative Investment Funds) have created new pools of capital.

This shift toward local capital deepens the ecosystem and makes it more resilient. It also allows for more patient; long-term investing aligned with India's structural growth.

9. Sectoral Themes Shaping Indian Private Equity

The Indian private equity market has distinct sectoral signatures, reflecting the country's economic structure and consumption patterns.

Financial Services has been the largest recipient of PE capital, driven by the growth of NBFCs, fintech, microfinance, digital payments, and private-sector banks.

Healthcare is another core sector, spanning hospitals, diagnostics, pharmaceuticals, biosimilars, and healthtech.

Consumer and Retail investments reflect India's rising incomes and evolving preferences.

IT and ITES, the backbone of Indian global competitiveness, continue to attract sustained interest.

Education, **logistics**, **manufacturing**, and **renewable energy** have all emerged as attractive themes, each with distinctive capital requirements and value creation models.

The diversity of India's economy ensures that private equity firms have a wide and varied opportunity set, from early-stage ventures to billion-dollar buyouts.

10. Governance, Regulation, and the Role of Government Policy

India's private equity market is heavily influenced by its regulatory environment. SEBI's reforms in corporate governance, disclosure norms, insider trading laws, and IPO processes strengthened investor confidence and made India's public markets among the most sophisticated in the world.

Regulations governing foreign direct investment (FDI), commercial banking, NBFCs, and capital markets shape transaction structures and investment strategies. While India's regulatory environment is often seen as complex, it has also contributed to stability and long-term market integrity.

Private equity firms must navigate these rules carefully, but the overall direction of policy - encouraging foreign investment, fostering entrepreneurship, digitizing government services - has been broadly supportive.

11. The Indian Private Equity Playbook: What Makes the Market Different

India's private equity market has several unique characteristics. Founder dynamics play a central role: promoters typically retain significant control, requiring careful alignment discussions, trust building, and governance negotiation. Minority rights, board representation, exit options, and shareholder agreements must be tailored to India's legal environment.

India also requires patience. Growth takes time, regulatory processes can be slow, and operational challenges arise from the country's geographic and socioeconomic diversity. Successful investors develop deep sector expertise, build local teams, and cultivate long-term relationships.

Another distinct feature is India's exit landscape. Unlike many emerging markets, India has robust public markets capable of absorbing large IPOs. Secondary sales, strategic M&A, and founder buybacks are also common exit paths. This diversity reduces risk and attracts global capital.

12. India's Digital Public Infrastructure: A Unique Accelerator

India's digital transformation is deeply intertwined with its private equity story. The national digital public infrastructure - Aadhaar for identity, UPI for payments, ONDC for e-commerce, DigiLocker for documentation, and GSTN for taxation - created a frictionless foundation for entrepreneurship.

These platforms lowered entry barriers, reduced compliance complexity, and enabled millions of Indians to participate in the digital economy. No other emerging market has created digital rails of comparable scale. For private equity investors, this means faster growth, broader addressable markets, and more scalable business models.

The rise of fintech, online education, e-commerce, mobility, healthtech, SaaS, and D2C brands would not have been possible without this infrastructure. India's digital ecosystem is a core competitive advantage in attracting global private capital.

13. Challenges and Constraints in the Indian Private Equity Market

Despite its promise, investing in India presents challenges. Regulatory unpredictability, lengthy legal processes, infrastructure bottlenecks, and complex tax rules can complicate transactions. The market is competitive, driving up valuations and compressing returns.

Additionally, governance issues remain a concern in certain segments. Investors must conduct thorough diligence on financial records, customer contracts, compliance processes, and management integrity. The cultural nuances of founder relationships, succession planning, and family ownership require specialized skill and sensitivity.

Macroeconomic volatility - including inflation, currency fluctuations, and global capital cycle sensitivity - can influence deal timing and exit outcomes. Despite these challenges, private equity firms with disciplined processes and local insight continue to outperform.

14. The Future of Private Equity in India

India is poised to become one of the world's largest private equity markets over the next two decades. The reasons are structural: a young population, rapid urbanization, expanding middle class, digital penetration, capital market depth, and institutional reforms.

Sectors like renewable energy, manufacturing, healthcare, consumer brands, EV infrastructure, logistics, and financial inclusion offer multibillion-dollar opportunities. The formalization of SMEs and the rise of domestic consumption will create new investable segments.

As India continues its journey toward becoming a multi-trillion-dollar economy, private equity will play a central role in financing growth, reshaping industries, professionalizing businesses, and driving innovation.

Conclusion: India's Private Equity Journey as a Story of Transformation

Private equity in India has grown from a marginal presence in the early 1990s into a core pillar of the nation's economic engine. It reflects India's evolution from a closed economy to a global investment destination, from a family-driven corporate landscape to a professionally managed ecosystem, and from incremental development to digital-first innovation.

The Indian private equity market is not merely an adaptation of Western models; it is a distinct blend of family enterprise, global capital, entrepreneurial ambition, and institutional reform. Its trajectory mirrors the broader story of India's economic rise - dynamic, complex, and filled with potential.

As we look ahead, India's private equity industry is positioned not only to grow but to shape the future of global investing. For investors with patience, insight, and local understanding, India will remain one of the most compelling frontiers of private capital in the 21st century.

CHAPTER 4 - CORE FINANCIAL CONCEPTS IN PRIVATE EQUITY

SECTION A

Valuation Foundations: Enterprise Value, EBITDA, Multiples, Discounted Cash Flow

Private equity investing is built on a foundation of financial analysis. No matter how compelling a business appears, how persuasive its management team sounds, or how exciting an industry trend looks, a private equity deal ultimately succeeds or fails based on one fundamental reality: **the price paid relative to the value received.**

This is why valuation sits at the heart of private equity. Unlike public markets, where prices fluctuate continuously and investors can exit instantly, private equity investments are illiquid and long-dated. You typically hold them for **5–7 years**, sometimes longer. There is no opportunity to "average down" or quickly exit a bad position. A single mistake in valuation can echo for years and destroy fund returns.

Because of this unforgiving structural reality, private equity firms rely on a set of valuation tools that help them understand:

- how much a company is worth today
- how much cash it can generate in the future
- what return they can make at exit
- and what risks might derail the investment

Section A explains these tools in a step-by-step, deeply explanatory manner.

---

1. Enterprise Value and Equity Value - The Two Lenses of Valuation

1.1 Why We Need Two Notions of Value

When valuing a business, private equity professionals distinguish between **enterprise value (EV)** and **equity value.** These concepts often confuse newcomers, but they are very logical when understood through the lens of ownership.

Think of a company as a house:

- *Enterprise value* is the value of the entire house.
- *Equity value* is the price you pay after deducting the outstanding mortgage.

The bank (debt) must be paid before the homeowner (equity) gets anything. The same logic applies to companies.

1.2 Formal Definition

Enterprise Value = value of the entire business to *all* capital providers

Equity Value = value belonging *only to shareholders*

1.3 The Formula

EV = Equity Value + Debt - Cash

Why?

- **Debt increases EV** because a buyer takes over the obligation to repay it.
- **Cash decreases EV** because cash reduces the effective purchase cost.

Or in words:

Enterprise Value = Price of shares + Amount needed to pay off lenders – Cash you receive when you buy the company.

This is why buyers often talk in EV terms while sellers think in equity terms.

1.4 Intuitive Example

Suppose a PE firm plans to buy 100% of a company.

- Negotiated equity price: ₹600 crore
- Company debt: ₹300 crore
- Company cash: ₹50 crore

As the buyer, you must:

- Pay ₹600 crore to the seller
- Take on the company's debt of ₹300 crore (you inherit this obligation)
- You get the company's cash balance of ₹50 crore (this reduces your effective outlay)

So, you are effectively paying:

```
600 + 300 - 50 = 850 crore
```

This ₹850 crore is the enterprise value.

It tells you: "The business, stripped of its financing, is worth ₹850 crore."

1.5 Why Private Equity Focuses on EV

EV helps separate:

- the *value of operations*

from
- the *way they were financed*

PE firms often heavily change the capital structure (add debt, refinance, etc.), so EV gives a better picture of the business itself, irrespective of financing.

1.6 India-Specific Complications

Indian companies often require more EV adjustments than Western firms because:

- promoter loans may be disguised as operating liabilities
- family salaries may not be market-based
- related-party transactions distort margins
- cash balances may not be fully available
- tax liabilities may be contingent

Therefore, determining true EV requires deep diligence.

---

2. EBITDA - The Starting Point for Measuring Operating Performance

2.1 Why PE Uses EBITDA Instead of Net Profit

Net profit (PAT) is heavily influenced by:

- interest
- depreciation
- amortization
- taxes
- capital structure
- accounting choices

But PE firms want to understand the company's **true operating performance** before these distortions. EBITDA cleans up these effects.

2.2 Formal Definition

EBITDA = Earnings Before Interest, Taxes, Depreciation, Amortization

This measures **cash operating profitability**.

2.3 Why Remove D&A?

Depreciation and amortization:

- are accounting charges
- do not involve cash leaving the business today
- depend on historical capex, not current performance

EBITDA therefore gives a "purer" measure of profits from running the business.

2.4 Normalizing EBITDA - One of the Most Critical PE Activities

PE firms almost *never* use reported EBITDA.

Why?

Because reported EBITDA may include:

- unusual items
- distortions
- family expenses
- non-operating income
- one-time events

A PE firm's job is to estimate **normalized EBITDA** - the EBITDA the business would generate under normal, recurring conditions.

2.5 Example (Explained Step-by-Step)

Reported EBITDA: ₹120 crore

Adjustments:

- Founder is underpaid relative to market by ₹10 crore. A new CEO will cost more. → Add back ₹10 crore
- Company received a one-time insurance payout of ₹5 crore → Remove it
- A discontinued product line lost ₹8 crore → Add back because it won't recur

```
Normalized EBITDA = 120 + 10 - 5 + 8 = 133 crore
```

This **₹133 crore** forms the foundation of valuation - not the reported ₹120 crore.

2.6 Why Normalization Is Especially Crucial in India

India's SME and promoter-driven corporate landscape often include:

- personal expenses running through business
- skimming of cash revenues
- family employees at non-market salaries
- old ERP systems with inconsistent data
- informal vendor/customer arrangements

Hence, determining true EBITDA requires deeper forensics.

---

3. Valuation Multiples - The Market-Based Anchor for Pricing

3.1 Why Multiples Exist

Private equity firms need to know:

"What do similar companies sell for today?"

Multiples provide this answer.

The most common is:

EV/EBITDA

This tells you how many times EBITDA the market is willing to pay for a business.

3.2 Why Use EBITDA Multiples Instead of P/E Ratios?

Because EBITDA:

- reflects operations, not financing
- works well for buyouts (where financing will change)
- is comparable across companies
- provides stable benchmarks

P/E ratios vary wildly because tax rates, capital structure, and accounting policies differ.

3.3 How Multiples Reflect Business Quality

A high multiple means:

- stable cash flows
- strong competitive position
- high growth prospects
- capable management
- scalable economics

A low multiple means:

- volatility
- commoditized products
- low margins
- high capex
- weak governance

3.4 Numerical Example: Applying a Multiple

If EBITDA = ₹133 crore

and industry multiple = 12×

EV = 12 × 133 = 1596 crore

To compute **equity value**, subtract net debt (₹250 crore):

Equity Value = 1596 - 250 = 1346 crore

This becomes our benchmark negotiation price.

3.5 Indian Multiples Tend to Be Unique

India often shows:

- **premium multiples** for digital, consumer, healthcare
- **discount multiples** for asset-heavy manufacturing
- **regional differences** in mid-market valuations
- **informal sector distortions** that complicate comparables

PE firms must therefore adjust multiples for India-specific realities.

4. Discounted Cash Flow (DCF) - Measuring Intrinsic Value

Multiples tell you "what the market pays."

DCF tells you **what the business is fundamentally worth.**

Both matter.

But DCF is more mathematically grounded and forces investors to think about the future cash the business will produce.

4.1 The DCF Framework

DCF valuation involves:

1. Projecting future free cash flows
2. Discounting them at an appropriate cost of capital
3. Calculating terminal value
4. Summing these components to get enterprise value

4.2 The Fundamental DCF Formula

$$EV = \sum_{t=1}^{n} \frac{FCF_t}{(1 + WACC)^t} + \frac{TV}{(1 + WACC)^n}$$

Where:

- FCF_t = Free Cash Flow in year t
- $WACC$ = Weighted Average Cost of Capital
- TV = Terminal Value

4.3 Why DCF Is Especially Important in PE

Private equity firms use DCF to:

- test valuation assumptions rigorously
- estimate downside scenarios
- build conviction in growth projections

- justify paying above-market multiples

A DCF forces discipline.

4.4 Free Cash Flow (FCF) - The Lifeblood of PE

FCF = EBITDA - Taxes - Capex - ΔWC

Every part has meaning:

- **EBITDA** = core earnings
- **Taxes** = cash taxes, not accounting tax
- **Capex** = necessary reinvestments
- **Δ Working Capital** = money stuck in receivables and inventory

In India, working capital is often a major drag on cash flow because many customers take long credit periods.

---

5. Full DCF Example - Explained in Slow, Detailed Steps

Assume:

- EBITDA starts at ₹150 crore
- EBITDA grows 10% annually
- Capex = ₹40 crore per year
- Taxes = 25% of EBITDA
- Working capital consumes ₹10 crore annually
- WACC = 12%
- Terminal multiple: 10× EV/EBITDA

Step 1: Project EBITDA

Year	EBITDA (₹ cr)	Explanation
1	150	Base year
2	165	+10%
3	181.5	Previous ×1.10
4	199.65	Previous ×1.10
5	219.62	Previous ×1.10

Step 2: Convert EBITDA to Free Cash Flow

For Year 1:

- Tax = 25% of 150 = 37.5
- Capex = 40
- Working capital = 10

$$FCF_1 = 150 - 40 - 37.5 - 10 = 62.5$$

Repeating:

Year	EBITDA	FCF
1	150	62.5
2	165	71.25
3	181.5	80.37
4	199.65	90.00
5	219.62	100.24

Step 3: Discount Each FCF

Using 12% discount rate:

$$PV_1 = 62.5/1.12 = 55.8$$

$$PV_2 = 71.25/1.12^2 = 56.8$$

...and so on.

Present value of 5-year FCF ≈ **₹302 crore.**

Step 4: Calculate Terminal Value

Terminal EBITDA = ₹219.62 crore

Terminal EV = $219.62 \times 10 = 2196$

Discount terminal value:

$$PV_{TV} = 2196/1.12^5 \approx 1245$$

Step 5: Final Enterprise Value

$$EV = 302 + 1245 = 1547 \text{ crore}$$

This becomes our DCF valuation.

---

6. When to Use Multiples vs When to Use DCF

Multiples are best when:

- industry has stable benchmarking
- company performance aligns with peers
- there are many comparable transactions
- investors need a quick valuation anchor

DCF is best when:

- business has unusual cash flow patterns
- working capital swings matter
- company is unique or lacks comps
- leverage or margin expansion will materially change the business

DCF is more work, but yields deeper conviction.

---

7. Sensitivity Analysis - Understanding Risk and Assumption Dependency

DCF outputs are extremely sensitive to small changes in assumptions.

Private equity firms therefore use **sensitivity tables** to understand valuation risk.

Example ASCII Sensitivity Table

EXIT MULTIPLE (x)

EBITDA 8x 10x 12x 14x

200 1600 2000 2400 2800

220 1760 2200 2640 3080

240 1920 2400 2880 3360

This helps ICs understand:

- worst-case valuation
- best-case valuation
- realistic mid-point

---

8. Combining All Methods - Triangulation

Private equity firms do not rely on just one method.

They triangulate:

- **DCF value**
- **Comparable company multiples**

- **Precedent transaction multiples**
- **Management projections sanity checks**
- **PE value creation potential**

The intersection of these ranges becomes the "valuation corridor."

SECTION B - Leverage, Returns, Capital Structure, IRR/MOIC, and LBO Mechanics

Private equity returns are built at the intersection of **finance, operations, and strategy**. Section A explained how valuation determines what a business is worth. Section B now explains **how private equity investors use capital structure, leverage, and cash flow to enhance returns**, and how those returns are measured quantitatively.

This section is intentionally detailed. It mirrors what a first-year PE associate learns in an intensive training program and what MBA programs introduce in advanced corporate finance electives. It blends mathematics, intuition, frameworks, and real-world logic - with specific applications to the Indian private equity environment.

---

1. The Essence of Leverage in Private Equity

1.1 Why Leverage Matters

The defining feature of a private equity buyout is **the use of debt** to acquire a company. Leverage magnifies returns because:

- the PE firm only invests a portion of the purchase price
- debt is cheaper than equity
- the firm keeps 100% of equity upside

This is similar to buying real estate with a mortgage: a small equity check controls a large asset.

1.2 How Leverage Boosts Returns

If a PE firm buys a ₹1,000 crore business with:

- ₹600 crore debt
- ₹400 crore equity

Then even a modest increase in enterprise value dramatically boosts equity returns.

Illustration (Simplified)

If EV grows from ₹1,000 crore to ₹1,200 crore:

- Debt = still ₹600 crore
- Equity now = 1,200 – 600 = ₹600 crore
- Equity grew from 400 → 600 = **50% gain**
- EV grew only **20%**

This is leverage at work.

1.3 Why Leverage Is Not Just About Higher Returns

Leverage is also a **discipline mechanism**:

- forces companies to generate cash
- prevents wasteful expansion
- aligns management with profitability
- speeds up operational improvements

This is why PE-backed companies often become more focused, efficient, and disciplined.

1.4 Indian Context: Historically Lower Leverage

India traditionally used lower leverage because:

- banks avoid financing buyouts
- regulations restricted leveraged lending
- promoter-owned companies avoided debt
- bankruptcy resolution was slow before IBC (2016)

However, with:

- private credit
- AIF structures
- offshore lending
- better insolvency frameworks

...leverage in India is increasing steadily.

2. Capital Structure Engineering - How PE Firms Design Debt

2.1 Capital Structure Components

Debt in PE deals usually includes:

1. **Senior secured loans** (lowest risk, lowest interest)
2. **Unitranche loans** (merged senior + mezzanine)
3. **Mezzanine or subordinated debt** (higher interest, flexible)
4. **Seller financing** (promoter roll-over)
5. **Preferred equity** (quasi-debt)
6. **Convertible instruments** (common in India)

2.2 What PE Firms Try to Optimize

The best capital structure:

- maximizes debt capacity
- minimizes interest burden
- avoids restrictive covenants

- ensures enough liquidity for growth
- protects the downside

PE firms often prefer:

- **fixed rate debt** in volatile interest markets
- **longer maturities** to avoid refinancing risk
- **covenant-lite structures** for flexibility

2.3 India-Specific Capital Structures

India frequently uses:

- NCDs (non-convertible debentures)
- structured credit
- CCDs (compulsorily convertible debentures)
- CCPS (compulsorily convertible preference shares)

These instruments navigate FDI norms and enable flexible payouts.

---

3. Debt Sizing - How Much Leverage a Deal Can Support

3.1 Debt Capacity Depends on Cash Flow

Debt sizing is mostly driven by:

- EBITDA
- cash conversion
- stability of earnings
- interest coverage ratios
- lender appetite
- asset base

3.2 Standard Leverage Ratios (Global vs India)

Market	Typical LBO Debt/EBITDA
U.S.	5.0–6.5×
Europe	4.5–6.0×
India	2.0–3.5×

Why is India lower?

- banks avoid funding buyouts
- higher interest rates
- more earnings volatility
- informal sector complexities
- slower receivable cycles

But private credit now supports **4–5× EBITDA** on select deals.

3.3 Interest Coverage Ratios

Lenders evaluate a company's ability to pay interest.

$$\text{Interest Coverage} = \frac{\text{EBITDA}}{\text{Interest Expense}}$$

Typical minimums:

- U.S.: 2.0×
- Europe: 2.5×
- India: 3.0–3.5×

Higher volatility → requires higher cushions.

---

4. Free Cash Flow (FCF) - The Lifeblood of Debt Repayment

4.1 Why FCF Matters More Than EBITDA

Debt is repaid with **cash**, not EBITDA.

Thus, PE firms analyze cash flow deeply:

```
FCF = EBITDA - Taxes - Capex - ΔWorking Capital
```

4.2 Why Working Capital Is Crucial in India

Indian businesses often have:

- long receivable cycles
- tight vendor payments
- high inventory needs
- complex distribution chains

As a result:

```
ΔWC is usually negative
```

This reduces free cash flow.

4.3 Case Example (Highly Explanatory)

A packaging company has:

- EBITDA = ₹150 crore
- Taxes = ₹35 crore
- Capex = ₹50 crore
- ΔWC = ₹20 crore (increase)

```
FCF = 150 - 35 - 50 - 20 = 45 crore
```

Only ₹45 crore is available for:

- debt repayment
- dividends
- reinvestment

If annual interest is >₹45 crore, the company cannot cover interest - so leverage must be reduced.

5. Internal Rate of Return (IRR) - Measuring Private Equity Performance

5.1 Why IRR Is the Most Important Metric

IRR measures the **annualized rate of return** on an investment. It incorporates:

- cash flows
- timing
- magnitude

This makes it superior to simple percentage returns.

5.2 Formal IRR Formula

$$0 = -I_0 + \frac{CF_1}{(1+r)^1} + \frac{CF_2}{(1+r)^2} + \dots + \frac{CF_n}{(1+r)^n}$$

Where:

- I_0 = initial investment
- CF_t = cash flow at time t
- r = IRR

IRR is the rate that sets NPV = 0.

5.3 Intuitive Understanding

IRR tells you:

"If I invested ₹100 today and received these cash flows over time, what annual return did I earn?"

It accounts for time value - receiving money earlier boosts IRR significantly.

5.4 Step-by-Step Numerical Example (Explained in Detail)

A PE fund invests **₹200 crore** today.

Cash flows:

- Year 1: ₹30 crore
- Year 2: ₹40 crore
- Year 3: ₹40 crore
- Year 4: ₹250 crore (exit)

Plug into IRR logic:

$$200 = \frac{30}{(1 + r)} + \frac{40}{(1 + r)^2} + \frac{40}{(1 + r)^3} + \frac{250}{(1 + r)^4}$$

Solving yields:

$$\text{IRR} \approx 22.7\%$$

Interpretation

The investment earned ~22.7% per year over four years.

6. MOIC (Multiple on Invested Capital)

6.1 Formula

$$\text{MOIC} = \frac{\text{Total Cash Returned}}{\text{Total Cash Invested}}$$

6.2 Example

If PE firm invests ₹200 crore and exits at ₹480 crore:

$$\text{MOIC} = \frac{480}{200} = 2.4 \times$$

Difference Between IRR and MOIC

- **MOIC** measures magnitude of return
- **IRR** measures speed of return

A 3× MOIC in 10 years is mediocre; a 3× MOIC in 3 years is exceptional.

---

7. The Three Drivers of Returns in Private Equity

PE firms break return creation into:

1. **Multiple expansion**
2. **Earnings growth**
3. **Debt paydown (deleveraging)**

7.1 Multiple Expansion

If you buy at 10× EBITDA and exit at 12×, value increases even without operational improvement.

7.2 Earnings Growth

If EBITDA grows from ₹100 crore to ₹200 crore, equity value doubles at the same multiple.

7.3 Debt Paydown

As debt reduces, equity value automatically increases.

7.4 Example - Decomposition

Buyout of an FMCG firm:

- Entry EV: ₹1,000 crore
- Entry EBITDA: ₹100 crore (10×)
- Exit EBITDA: ₹150 crore
- Exit multiple: 11×
- Exit EV: ₹1,650 crore
- Debt paydown: ₹300 → ₹100 crore

Equity value grows from:

```
1000 - 300 = 700
```

to:

```
1650 - 100 = 1550
```

Gain = 850 crore.

Breakdown:

- EBITDA growth contributed: 500 crore
- Multiple expansion contributed: 150 crore
- Deleveraging contributed: 200 crore

---

8. LBO Mechanics - Connecting All the Concepts

8.1 LBO Overview

A Leveraged Buyout (LBO) model simulates:

- purchase price
- capital structure

- debt schedule
- cash flows
- exit valuation
- equity returns (IRR, MOIC)

8.2 The Goal of LBO Modelling

To answer:

"If we buy this company with this much debt, and grow it this much, what return do we earn?"

8.3 Core Components of an LBO Model

1. **Sources & Uses** of funds
2. **Debt schedule** (repayment mechanics)
3. **Operating model**
4. **Free cash flow**
5. **Exit valuation**
6. **Returns analysis**

---

9. Mini-LBO Case Study - Step-by-Step

A private equity firm wants to buy a specialty chemicals company.

9.1 Purchase Price

- EV = ₹1,200 crore
- Net debt = ₹200 crore
- Equity = ₹1,000 crore

9.2 Capital Structure

PE plans to finance:

- Debt: ₹600 crore
- Equity: ₹400 crore

9.3 Operating Performance

Current EBITDA = ₹150 crore

EBITDA grows 8% per year.

9.4 Cash Flow Assumptions

- Capex = 30 crore/year
- Working capital = 10 crore/year
- Tax rate = 25%
- Interest on debt = 12%

9.5 Year-by-Year Free Cash Flow Calculation

Year 1 EBITDA:

```
150 × 1.08 = 162
```

Taxes = 25% × 162 = 40.5

FCF = EBITDA – capex – taxes – ΔWC

= 162 – 30 – 40.5 – 10

= 81.5 crore

Year 2,3,4,5 follow similarly.

9.6 Debt Repayment Schedule

Assume annual repayment = **₹60 crore**.

ASCII representation:

Debt Balance (₹ crore)

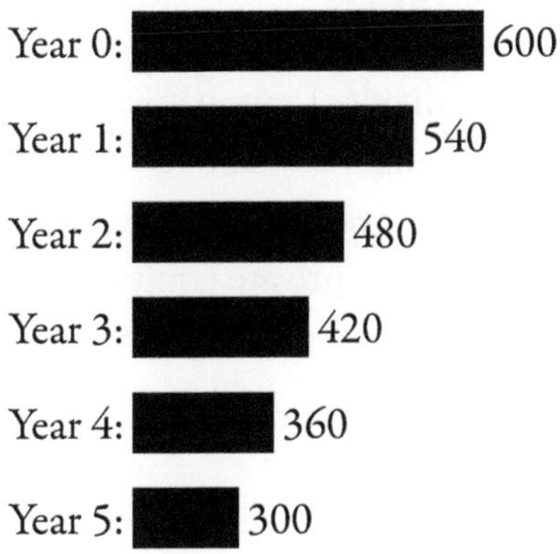

9.7 Exit After 5 Years

- Exit EBITDA = 150 × 1.08^5 ≈ 220 crore
- Exit multiple = 11×
- Exit EV = 220 × 11 = 2,420 crore
- Debt remaining = 300 crore

Equity at exit = 2,420 – 300 = 2,120 crore

9.8 Returns

Initial equity = 400 crore

Final equity = 2,120 crore

$$\text{MOIC} = \frac{2120}{400} = 5.3\times$$

$$\text{IRR} \approx 40.2\%$$

This is an outstanding PE return.

SECTION C - Portfolio Construction, Exit Mechanics, Risk Management, and Full Indian Buyout Case Study

Private equity is not only about valuing individual companies; it is also about constructing a portfolio, managing risk, and achieving predictable returns across an entire fund. Section C integrates everything from Sections A and B and shows how private equity firms apply financial concepts in real-world investments, with deep emphasis on the Indian market.

---

1. Portfolio Construction in Private Equity

1.1 Why Portfolio Construction Matters

A private equity fund is not one investment - it is a **portfolio of 8–20 companies**.

The goal is to achieve consistent, risk-adjusted returns **for the fund as a whole**, not just one deal.

Every PE fund needs to answer:

- How many deals should we make?
- How concentrated should the fund be?
- How do we diversify by sector, geography, stage, or risk profile?
- What size of equity checks should we target?

Incorrect portfolio construction can destroy returns even if individual deals perform well.

1.2 Concentration vs Diversification

High Concentration Advantages

- higher conviction deals
- deeper operational involvement
- potentially higher returns
- lower administrative burden

Risks

- one bad deal can severely depress fund returns
- lack of diversification amplifies sector shocks
- exit risk concentrated in fewer assets

High Diversification Advantages

- smoother fund-level returns
- lower risk per investment
- broader exposure to economic cycles

Risks

- difficulty in adding value to many companies
- smaller equity positions → smaller upside
- operational resource constraints

Standard Practice

Most mid-market PE funds follow:

- **10–15 platform deals**
- **Concentration limit**: no single deal > 15% of the fund
- **Sector limit**: no sector > 30% of the fund

---

2. Diversification Dimensions in Private Equity

PE firms diversify along four primary axes.

2.1 By Sector

Typical PE exposure mix in India:

Consumer/retail 20%

Healthcare 15%

Financial services 25%

Technology/SaaS 10%

Industrial 15%

Others 5–10%

Diversification reduces:

- regulatory shocks
- sector cycles
- margin swings
- technology obsolescence

2.2 By Geography

Even within India, geography matters due to:

- consumer preference differences
- regulatory variations
- infrastructure quality
- supply chain access

PE firms often prefer:

- Western India (Gujarat, Maharashtra) for manufacturing
- South India (Karnataka, Tamil Nadu) for technology
- North India for consumer/retail scale

2.3 By Stage

Funds often blend:

- buyouts (safer cash flows)
- growth equity (higher upside)
- structured credit
- selective venture investments

This smooths fund-level IRR.

2.4 By Holding Period

Not all investments exit in year 5.

A staggered exit base prevents "bunching risk" where many assets depend on the same market cycle.

---

3. Exit Routes - The Realization of PE Value

Exits are the single most important events for private equity firms. They determine actual returns and whether LPs receive distributable cash.

3.1 IPO (Initial Public Offering)

Why IPOs Are Appealing

- highest multiples
- liquidity
- prestige for founders
- retention of ownership for management

Why They Are Difficult

- heavy regulatory burden
- market-timing risk
- dependency on retail appetite
- promoter governance scrutiny

India's equity markets - especially after 2020 - became much more receptive to PE-backed IPOs.

3.2 Strategic Sales

A strategic buyer pays for:

- synergies
- capabilities
- distribution expansion
- defensive positioning

These exits often command **premium multiples.**

3.3 Secondary Sales

Private equity-to-private equity sales are now very common in India.

Example:

Advent buying stakes from Warburg Pincus, KKR selling to BPEA EQT, etc.

Reasons:

- clean transactions
- buyer understands PE governance
- aligned expectations

- faster execution

3.4 Promoter Buybacks

Common in India due to family ownership.

Advantages:

- easiest execution
- promoters know the business
- avoids public disclosure

But valuation negotiations can be tough.

3.5 Recap/Dividend Recapitalization

PE firms sometimes borrow more debt and take a dividend before exiting.

This boosts IRR but increases leverage risk.

---

4. Advanced Return Sensitivity and Scenario Modelling

PE firms run **hundreds of scenarios** before investment committee approval.

Key variables include:

- revenue growth
- EBITDA margins
- exit multiple
- debt repayment speed
- interest rate changes
- working capital cycles

4.1 Example - IRR Sensitivity to Exit EBITDA

Assume:

- purchase EBITDA = 100
- exit multiple = 10×
- entry multiple = 10×
- debt constant
- equity = ₹500 crore

ASCII table:

Exit EBITDA Exit EV Equity Value MOIC IRR (5 yr)

80 (-20%) 800 300 0.6× -12%

100 (base) 1000 500 1.0× 0%

120 (+20%) 1200 700 1.4× 7.3%

150 (+50%) 1500 1000 2.0× 14.9%

200 (+100%) 2000 1500 3.0× 24.6%

Interpretation:

- Even a 20% decrease destroys returns.
- Upside is nonlinear beyond 50%.

4.2 Exit Multiple Sensitivity

Exit Multiple Exit EV (₹ cr) MOIC IRR (5 yr)

8× 800 0.6× -12%

10× 1000 1.0× 0%

12× 1200 1.4× 7%

14× 1400 1.8× 11%

4.3 Interest Rate Sensitivity

Increasing interest rates by 2% can reduce FCF by 20–35% in highly leveraged deals.

---

5. Full-Length Indian Buyout Case Study - 30+ Step, End-to-End Walkthrough

This is the most comprehensive part of Section C.

It walks through the entire lifecycle of a private equity deal:

- sourcing
- valuation
- capital structure
- debt modelling
- cash flow forecasting
- exit economics
- IRR/MOIC
- sensitivity analysis

CASE STUDY: Buyout of "Bharat Nutraceuticals Ltd."

An Indian mid-market FMCG company

Step 1 - Company Overview

- Category: Nutraceuticals & functional foods
- Revenue: ₹900 crore
- EBITDA: ₹150 crore (16.7% margin)
- Growth: 12% CAGR

- Capex: ₹35 crore/year
- Working capital: 12% of revenue

Strong brand, national distribution, asset-light manufacturing.

Step 2 - Investment Thesis

PE firm believes it can:

- expand distribution
- launch digital-first D2C channels
- improve gross margins
- reduce working capital drag
- introduce new product lines
- expand export channels

Step 3 - Initial Valuation Using EV/EBITDA

Sector multiple: **12×**

EV = 12 × 150 = 1800 crore

Promoter debt: 200

Cash: 50

Net Debt = 200 - 50 = 150
Equity = 1800 - 150 = 1650 crore

Step 4 - Negotiation Outcome

PE firm negotiates:

Final Enterprise Value: ₹1,750 crore

Step 5 - Capital Structure

Debt: ₹900 crore

Equity: ₹850 crore

Leverage = 6× EBITDA (aggressive, but FMCG cash flows are strong)

Step 6 - Interest & Debt Terms

- Senior debt: 11%
- Mezzanine debt: 15%
- Weighted cost: 12.3%
- Annual amortization: ₹120 crore

Step 7 - Operating Projections (5 Years)

Revenue grows 12% CAGR

EBITDA margin improves from 16.7% → 20%

Summary:

Year EBITDA (₹ cr)

1 168

2 188

3 211

4 236

5 265

Step 8 - Free Cash Flow

Compute for Year 1:

- EBITDA = 168
- Tax = 25% = 42
- Capex = 35
- ΔWC = 12% of ΔRevenue
- ΔRevenue = 108 crore → WC increase = 13 crore

FCF_1 = 168 - 42 - 35 - 13 = 78 crore

Similar calculations produce:

Year	FCF (₹ cr)
1	78
2	92
3	108
4	127
5	149

Step 9 - Debt Repayment Schedule

Year	Opening Debt	Repayment	Closing Debt
0	900	-	900
1	900	120	780
2	780	120	660
3	660	120	540
4	540	120	420

5 420 120 300

ASCII chart:

Debt Balance Over Time

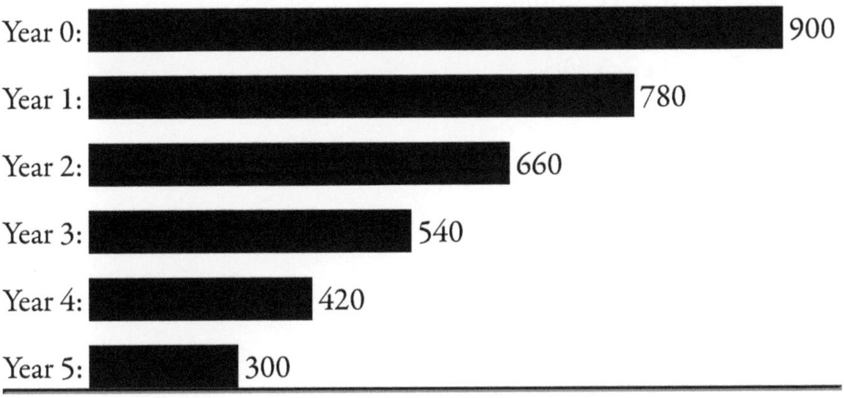

Step 10 - Exit Year Calculations

Exit EBITDA = **₹265 crore**

Exit multiple = **14×** (higher due to margin expansion)

```
Exit EV = 265 × 14 = 3710 crore
```

Debt remaining = 300 crore

Equity proceeds = 3710 - 300 = **₹3,410 crore**

Step 11 - Returns

Initial equity = ₹850 crore

Final equity = ₹3410 crore

$$\text{MOIC} = \frac{3410}{850} = 4.0\times$$

$$\text{IRR} \approx 33\%$$

Step 12 - Sensitivity Tables

Exit Multiple Sensitivity

12× 14× 16×

EV 3180 3710 4240

Equity 2880 3410 3940

MOIC 3.4× 4.0× 4.6×

IRR 28% 33% 37%

EBITDA Sensitivity

EBITDA Exit EV (14×) Equity IRR

240 3360 3060 29%

265 3710 3410 33%

300 4200 3900 37%

Step 13 - Return Decomposition

- **EBITDA growth contribution:** +1800 crore
- **Multiple expansion contribution:** +600 crore
- **Deleveraging contribution:** +350 crore

Step 14 - Investment Committee Takeaways

- Attractive base case: 33% IRR
- Downside case protected due to FMCG resilience
- Upside case driven by export strategy
- Leverage sustainable
- Strong cash flow profile

Conclusion of Section C

Section C ties together valuation, leverage, free cash flow, sensitivity analysis, and portfolio construction into a comprehensive framework for understanding how private equity firms:

- build conviction
- manage risk
- structure capital
- grow companies
- engineer exits
- deliver fund-level returns

You now have the full working knowledge of the **financial engine of private equity**, from foundational valuation to advanced buyout modelling.

CHAPTER 5 - TYPES OF PRIVATE EQUITY INVESTMENTS

Although private equity is often spoken of as if it were a single, unified discipline, the reality is far richer and more diverse. The term "private equity" describes a broad constellation of investment strategies that deploy capital into privately held companies at different stages of their development, under different market conditions, and with different objectives. These strategies span the lifecycle of a company -from the moment its founding team sketches an idea on a whiteboard, to the period of rapid growth that tests its organizational mettle, to the maturity stage when discipline and efficiency matter more than experimentation, and even to moments of crisis when a company's survival is at risk. Understanding these investment types is crucial because each one operates with distinct logics, return expectations, governance approaches, and risk profiles. A venture capitalist assessing a three-month-old startup and a buyout investor evaluating a forty-year-old industrial business are both part of private equity, yet they inhabit fundamentally different intellectual and operational worlds.

This chapter examines the major categories of private equity capital in a deeply descriptive, narrative manner. Rather than presenting the strategies as static definitions, it explores their underlying philosophies, the kinds of companies they target, the way investors behave within each strategy, and the reasons these approaches exist in the first place. It also situates each strategy within the global and Indian context, illustrating how the evolution of markets, technology, regulation, and entrepreneurship has shaped the role of these various forms of private capital.

Venture Capital: Financing Ideas Before They Become Industries

Venture capital is the most imaginative and forward-looking branch of private equity. It emerged in the twentieth century as a way to channel capital toward ideas that traditional financial institutions found too uncertain or unconventional. Banks and conservative investors typically demand collateral, predictable cash flows, and tangible assets. Startups, by their very nature, possess none of these things. They offer something far more volatile and far more powerful: the possibility of exponential value creation.

At its core, venture capital represents the willingness of investors to finance innovation long before its commercial outcomes can be predicted. The work of a venture capitalist involves making judgments about founders, technologies, and markets at embryonic stages, when data is sparse and uncertainty is immense. A VC is often betting on the quality of the idea and, even more importantly, the qualities of the founder -their resilience, their insight into a market, their ability to recruit and inspire talent, and their capacity to learn faster than the competition. In venture capital, the entrepreneur is often the central figure, and the investor's role is to amplify the potential that the founding team already embodies.

Venture capital evolved into a distinct asset class because innovation has become the engine of the modern economy. Companies like Apple, Amazon, Google, Facebook, Swiggy, and Flipkart all emerged from this ecosystem. The returns from a successful venture investment are nonlinear; a single company that achieves massive scale can pay for dozens of others that fail. Venture returns follow what statisticians call a "power law," meaning that a very small number of investments generate the overwhelming majority of the profits. This is why venture capital funds invest in large portfolios -they must accept failure as part of the model, knowing that the few successes will compensate for the many losses.

The Indian venture capital landscape has grown dramatically over the last fifteen years. The arrival of inexpensive mobile data, widespread smartphone adoption, national digital infrastructure like UPI, and a young population willing to experiment with new products have together created fertile ground for startup formation. As a result, India has become one of the world's largest startup ecosystems, producing unicorns in sectors ranging from food delivery to fintech to direct-to-consumer brands. Venture capital now plays a central role in the country's economic modernization, enabling founders to scale ideas quickly and decisively.

Growth Equity: Scaling Businesses That Have Proven Their Potential

As companies move beyond their early experiments and begin to demonstrate consistent revenue growth, predictable customer behavior, and scalable economics, they often require a different kind of capital -one that is less about betting on potential and more about accelerating already proven momentum. Growth equity fills this gap. It represents private equity investments in companies that have outgrown the uncertainties of the startup phase but are not yet mature enough to be considered stable, cash-generating enterprises in the buyout sense.

Growth equity investors look for businesses that have reached a point where the fundamentals are sound but where additional capital can produce disproportionately large improvements. These firms typically have strong unit economics, expanding customer bases, and demonstrated product-market fit. They may require funding to open new markets, expand production capacity, strengthen their leadership teams, invest in technology, or pursue acquisitions. The investor's role here is not to repair a broken company nor to encourage risky experimentation but rather to provide the capital and expertise that allow the company to scale faster and more efficiently than it could on its own.

Unlike venture capitalists, growth equity investors demand a high level of financial discipline. They expect reliable financial reporting, clear profitability pathways, and operational rigor. Yet they embrace more risk and higher growth potential than traditional buyout investors. Growth equity represents a sweet spot -where risk is moderate, growth potential is high, and the investor's ability to influence outcomes remains meaningful even without majority control.

India's growth equity market is one of the most active in the world. The country's fast-expanding consumer base, robust financial services sector, and globally competitive IT and pharma industries have made it a prime destination for growth-stage investments. International investors like General Atlantic, Warburg Pincus, KKR, and ChrysCapital have built deep portfolios across Indian companies that were already successful but still had large untapped markets to conquer. Growth equity thus plays a pivotal role in transforming mid-sized Indian businesses into national or international leaders.

Buyouts: Controlling Companies to Transform Their Trajectory

Buyouts represent the most established and disciplined form of private equity investing. In a buyout, the investor acquires a controlling stake in a company -often using significant leverage -and assumes the responsibility of driving its strategic direction. Buyout investing is grounded in the belief that many companies underperform not because of flawed business models, but because of inefficiencies, lack of professional management, suboptimal capital allocation, or insufficient strategic clarity. When a private equity firm takes control, it gains the authority to make the changes necessary to unleash the company's full potential.

The buyout model became globally dominant because it aligns capital, control, and incentives in a powerful way. When private equity investors take charge of a mature business, they do so with a clear plan to improve operations, streamline costs, professionalize governance, and accelerate revenue growth. These improvements may involve upgrading management teams, modernizing supply chains, digitizing processes, entering new markets, or divesting non-core assets. Buyout firms are known for their intense focus on key value-creation levers, often supported by operational specialists who partner with management teams to execute large-scale transformations.

A distinctive feature of buyout investing is the use of leverage. Because buyout targets are typically companies with stable cash flows and predictable margins, they can support debt. This leverage amplifies returns for equity holders -when the company grows or becomes more efficient, the equity portion expands dramatically once debt obligations are satisfied. Understanding leverage therefore requires a deep appreciation of capital structure engineering, debt repayment dynamics, and cash flow modelling, topics explored extensively in Chapter 4.

In India, buyouts have grown sharply over the last decade. Historically, they were rare because Indian businesses were often family-owned, promoters were reluctant to cede control, and banks were hesitant to lend against cash flows for acquisitions. Over time, however, generational transitions, corporate restructurings, divestitures by multinational corporations, and the rise of private credit have expanded the buyout landscape. Today, global firms such as Blackstone, KKR, Advent, Bain, Carlyle, and Baring Asia are active buyers of Indian companies across consumer, healthcare, IT services, pharmaceuticals, and manufacturing. Buyouts have thus become a major force in modernizing India's mid-to-large-scale corporate sector.

Distressed and Special Situations: Investing in Complexity and Crisis

Distressed investing represents a very different branch of private equity -one that operates at the intersection of finance, law, and turnaround management. Distressed investors deploy capital in situations where a company is facing financial stress, operational breakdowns, or insolvency. These investments exist because businesses often reach points where traditional financing is no longer available, creditors become impatient, and management teams face overwhelming challenges. Yet beneath the surface, many of these companies still possess valuable assets, brands, or market positions that can be revived with the right combination of capital, restructuring expertise, and legal navigation.

Distressed investors typically purchase debt at significant discounts or inject new capital into companies undergoing formal resolution processes. The investor's objective is to restructure the balance sheet, stabilize operations, and eventually return the business to profitability. This requires understanding not only the economics of the business but also the legal frameworks that govern creditor rights, insolvency proceedings, and asset recoveries.

In India, the distressed landscape changed dramatically after the introduction of the Insolvency and Bankruptcy Code (IBC) in 2016. For the first time in Indian history, creditors gained a predictable and time-bound mechanism to resolve insolvency cases. Major industrial assets like Essar Steel, Bhushan Steel, and Electrosteel Steels changed hands through the IBC process, attracting global investors with restructuring expertise. Special situations funds -such as Ares SSG, Värde Partners, Brookfield, and Edelweiss Alternatives -became major players by blending legal acumen with financial engineering. This segment of private equity thrives in complexity and rewards patience, precision, and risk tolerance.

Turnaround Investing: Reviving Companies on the Brink

Turnaround investing focuses on companies that are operationally broken but fundamentally salvageable. Unlike distressed investors, who often enter through creditor positions, turnaround investors typically inject equity capital and engage deeply with operations. These companies may be suffering from years of mismanagement, inefficient processes, outdated technology, or flawed strategies. The challenge is not simply to fix the balance sheet but to reform how the business operates on a day-to-day basis.

Turnaround professionals often begin by implementing leadership changes. They introduce seasoned executives who bring discipline, clarity, and structure to decision-making. They analyze the product portfolio, shedding unprofitable divisions and focusing resources on high-potential segments. They scrutinize working capital cycles, renegotiate vendor contracts, optimize pricing, and establish rigorous cost controls. Successful turnaround strategies require decisive action, hands-on involvement, and the willingness to make tough decisions quickly.

In India, many turnaround opportunities emerge in traditional sectors such as manufacturing, textiles, auto components, and engineering -industries that struggled to adapt to global competition and technological change. These companies often possess valuable assets, strong customer relationships, or deep domain knowledge but have suffered from outdated systems or weak governance. Turnaround investing remains a specialized and demanding field, but one that can produce significant returns when executed skillfully.

PIPEs: Private Capital Entering Public Markets

While private equity primarily focuses on privately held companies, it often engages with listed companies through a mechanism known as Private Investment in Public Equity (PIPE). In a PIPE transaction, a PE firm purchases a substantial stake in a publicly traded company, usually through a negotiated deal that provides capital directly to the company rather than through stock market transactions.

PIPEs appeal to private equity investors for several reasons. They allow investors to deploy large amounts of capital quickly, participate in the governance and strategic direction of high-quality listed companies, and sometimes pave the way for eventual buyouts or delistings. For companies, PIPE investments offer a way to raise capital without the delays and volatility associated with public offerings.

In India, PIPE investments have played a significant role in banking, financial services, pharmaceuticals, and consumer-facing sectors. PE firms often enter at moments when companies need growth capital, regulatory capital, or balance sheet strengthening. These deals blend the discipline of private equity with the transparency and scale of public markets.

Secondaries: Creating Liquidity in an Illiquid Asset Class

Private equity funds are long-dated vehicles, typically lasting ten years or more. However, many investors -known as limited partners (LPs) -may need liquidity sooner. Secondary transactions emerged as a solution to this problem. In a secondary sale, an LP sells its stake in an existing private equity fund to another investor. This creates a secondary market for private equity interests, allowing LPs to manage their portfolios more dynamically.

In recent years, a related category known as GP-led secondaries has gained prominence. In these transactions, the private equity firm (the general partner or GP) restructures or extends ownership of one or more portfolio companies by creating a continuation fund. This enables the GP to hold high-performing assets longer, while offering liquidity to outgoing investors. Secondaries have expanded rapidly because they provide flexibility in an asset class that is otherwise extremely illiquid.

Infrastructure and Real Assets: Investing in Stability and Nation-Building

Infrastructure investing represents the most stable and long-duration side of private markets. Unlike venture capital or buyouts, infrastructure assets provide essential services -transportation, energy, data connectivity, logistics -and often operate under long-term contracts or regulated pricing. The cash flows from infrastructure investments are typically predictable and steady, resembling bonds more than traditional equity investments.

Infrastructure investors evaluate assets such as highways, airports, power plants, renewable energy portfolios, transmission lines, water utilities, data centers, and fiber networks. These assets require substantial upfront capital but produce stable returns for decades. The role of an infrastructure investor involves analyzing concession agreements, regulatory frameworks, demand forecasts, and long-term maintenance obligations.

In India, infrastructure investing has flourished due to government initiatives, economic growth, and rising private sector participation. Global players like Brookfield, Macquarie, GIP, and I Squared Capital have invested billions into Indian roads, renewable energy platforms, data centers, and urban infrastructure. This category of private equity plays a critical role in nation-building by enabling large-scale physical and digital infrastructure development.

Private Credit: The New Engine Behind Modern Private Markets

Although private credit is not technically a form of private equity, it has become an indispensable part of the private markets ecosystem. Private credit funds lend directly to companies, filling gaps left by banks that face regulatory constraints. These funds provide acquisition financing, growth capital, mezzanine loans, structured financing, and rescue capital.

Private credit has grown rapidly in India as traditional lenders have become more cautious. Private credit funds offer flexible structures, quicker execution, and willingness to finance situations that banks avoid. They often secure collateral and earn high interest rates, delivering attractive risk-adjusted returns. This strategy has become a vital enabler of buyouts, recapitalizations, and special situations investments in India.

Conclusion: A Spectrum of Capital, Each Serving a Unique Purpose

The world of private equity is best understood not as a monolith but as a spectrum of capital strategies that collectively fuel business creation, growth, transformation, and recovery. Venture capital finances the boldest experiments at the frontier of innovation. Growth equity propels companies that have proven themselves but need capital to scale. Buyouts reshape and professionalize mature businesses, turning inefficiencies into opportunities. Distressed and turnaround strategies rescue companies in crisis, restoring value where others see only decline. Infrastructure investing builds the physical and digital backbone of economies. Private credit ensures that capital flows even when traditional lenders hesitate, supporting transactions across the private markets landscape.

By understanding these strategies not as isolated definitions but as interconnected responses to different corporate needs, one gains a holistic view of the private equity universe. Each strategy plays a distinct and essential role in shaping industries, enabling entrepreneurship, and driving economic development -particularly in dynamic markets like India, where the fusion of technology, demographics, and capital is reshaping the business landscape at an unprecedented pace.

CHAPTER 6 - VALUE CREATION IN PRIVATE EQUITY

Private equity is often misunderstood by casual observers. Outsiders imagine it as a form of financial alchemy dependent entirely on leverage: a process in which investors simply borrow money to acquire companies and rely on debt-fuelled financial engineering to amplify equity returns. While leverage plays a role, and while capital structure matters, the reality of modern private equity is far more complex, sophisticated, and operationally grounded. At its core, private equity is a craft of **value creation**. It is the art and science of transforming companies -sometimes radically, sometimes subtly -but always with the intent of making them healthier, more profitable, more strategic, more disciplined, and ultimately more valuable.

Value creation is what distinguishes exceptional private equity firms from mediocre ones. It is what separates a passive financial investor from an active owner. And it is the single greatest determinant of long-term private equity performance. This chapter explores, in a deeply descriptive and narrative fashion, the multifaceted ways in which private equity firms create value. It traces the evolution of value creation from the early days of the industry, when financial engineering dominated, to the present era, where operational excellence, strategic repositioning, digital transformation, and human capital enhancement define success. It also examines how value creation plays out in the Indian market, where unique cultural, structural, and regulatory factors shape the tools and approaches that investors must use.

The Evolution of Value Creation: From Financial Engineering to Operational Mastery

To understand value creation in private equity, one must begin with its historical evolution. In the 1980s and early 1990s, buyout firms operated in a world where financial engineering was the predominant lever of value. Interest rates were high, corporate structures were inefficient, and many public companies carried underutilized assets or bloated balance sheets. Private equity firms exploited this inefficiency by adding leverage, optimizing capital structures, and relying on rising equity markets to produce attractive returns. Debt was not merely a tool; it was the central thesis.

As financial markets matured and the industry globalized, this model changed. By the early 2000s, competition among private equity firms intensified. The easy wins from leverage and capital structure optimization diminished. Meanwhile, companies became more sophisticated, information became more accessible, and corporate governance standards improved. Simply buying a company and adding debt was no longer enough to drive returns. Investors had to find new ways to create value, and the industry's focus shifted from financial structuring to **operational excellence**.

By the 2010s, this transition had fully taken root. Private equity firms hired operating partners -experts in supply chains, pricing, digital transformation, lean manufacturing, marketing, and technology -from the world's best companies and consultancies. Funds built specialized teams dedicated to data analytics, procurement optimization, pricing science, and digital transformation. They embedded performance improvement playbooks into their processes. Value creation became a disciplined, systematic, multi-year undertaking, supported by frameworks, data, and hands-on engagement.

Today's private equity playbook is far more nuanced than anything imagined in the industry's early decades. Modern value creation blends financial discipline with operational rigor, strategic foresight, and cultural transformation. It emphasizes not just what a company does but how it behaves, how fast it learns, how well it allocates resources, how effectively it uses technology, and how strongly it aligns talent with priorities. And it does all of this under the unifying requirement of delivering measurable improvements in performance during a defined investment horizon.

Understanding the Drivers of Value: A Holistic Perspective

When a private equity firm acquires a company, it faces a simple, central question: *How can this business be worth more in five years than it is today?* The answers fall into several broad categories, all overlapping and interdependent. But instead of presenting them as a list, it is more insightful to understand them as intertwined conceptual pillars.

The first pillar is **revenue growth** -the most direct and often the most powerful driver of value. A company that grows its revenue base faster than its cost base expands its margins, improves its cash flow, and commands a higher valuation multiple. Private equity firms pursue revenue growth by helping companies enter new geographies, expand into adjacent product categories, strengthen their sales forces, improve distribution, or shift toward premium segments. Growth is not merely about selling more; it is about selling better, reaching the right customers, and capturing more value from every transaction.

A second pillar is **margin expansion**, achieved by reducing costs, improving efficiency, and optimizing operations. Many companies operate with inefficient cost structures -not because management is negligent, but because legacy systems, accumulated bureaucracy, and old habits create inertia. Private equity firms bring fresh eyes and data-driven scrutiny. They implement zero-based budgeting, renegotiate supplier contracts, redesign manufacturing workflows, and apply lean methodologies. Each incremental improvement -whether in procurement, logistics, marketing spend, or plant utilization -enhances profitability and frees cash for reinvestment or debt reduction.

A third pillar is **capital efficiency**, which focuses on how effectively a company deploys its financial resources. Even profitable companies may have poorly managed working capital, bloated inventories, inefficient receivable cycles, or misaligned capex priorities. Private equity investors bring discipline to capital allocation, insisting that every rupee invested generate a clearly measurable return. They design working capital dashboards, optimize purchasing terms, accelerate receivable collections, and evaluate capital expenditure through rigorous hurdle-rate analyses. As capital is freed from operational inefficiency, it can be redeployed into growth initiatives or used to reduce leverage.

A fourth pillar is **multiple expansion**, which occurs when the market views the company as fundamentally more attractive at exit than it was at entry. Multiple expansion is not purely financial magic; it is the natural by-product of transforming a business so that it occupies a superior competitive position. A company with a strong brand, a clear strategy, a professional management team, and a predictable cash flow stream commands a higher valuation multiple than one with inconsistent performance or weak governance. Private equity firms actively engineer this repositioning through governance improvements, strategic clarity, digital upgrades, and organizational strengthening.

The fifth pillar is **deleveraging** -the mechanical reduction of debt over the life of the investment. As the company generates cash, it repays loans and strengthens its balance sheet. Even if operational performance remains steady, deleveraging alone increases the equity value because the company's obligations shrink while its enterprise value holds constant or grows. In markets like India, where working capital cycles are often inefficient and debt markets are more conservative, deleveraging plays a particularly important role in value creation.

Together, these five pillars form the multi-dimensional framework through which private equity firms view every portfolio company. In practice, they overlap constantly. Growth drives margins. Margin improvements generate cash. Better cash flows reduce debt. Lower leverage reduces risk and enhances multiples. A well-positioned company opens new growth avenues. And the cycle reinforces itself.

Strategic Repositioning: Transforming a Company's Trajectory

One of the most powerful tools in the private equity value-creation arsenal is **strategic repositioning**. Many companies suffer not from a lack of execution, but from a lack of clarity about what they should be doing in the first place. Markets shift, technologies evolve, competitors emerge, and customer preferences change. A company that once grew rapidly may stagnate, not because its employees became less competent, but because its strategy failed to evolve.

Private equity firms bring perspective that internal teams may lack. They view the business through an external lens, comparing it to other players in the sector, studying global best practices, and evaluating long-term market trends. They ask fundamental questions: Should the company continue operating in all its current segments? Should it exit certain markets? Should it double down on its most profitable lines? Should it invest more aggressively in technology? Should it pursue vertical integration or shift toward asset-light models?

Strategic repositioning often involves reframing how a company defines itself. A packaging company may discover that its true competitive edge lies in supply-chain integration rather than simple manufacturing. A pharmaceutical company may realize that biosimilars offer higher long-term value than generic formulations. A consumer brand may learn that its path to scale lies in e-commerce rather than traditional retail. These strategic insights reshape resource allocation, organizational priorities, and investment decisions.

Private equity firms excel at catalyzing such strategic transformations because they combine capital, urgency, and outside perspective. Unlike internal management teams, who must navigate organisational politics and legacy constraints, private equity owners have both the authority and the discipline to implement bold changes. Their time horizon -typically four to seven years -forces clarity. They cannot postpone difficult decisions, nor can they entertain vague or unfocused strategies. Strategy under private equity ownership becomes sharper, bolder, and more disciplined.

Operational Excellence: The Heart of Modern Value Creation

While strategy sets direction, operations determine performance. Over the last twenty years, operational improvement has become the cornerstone of private equity value creation. Leading firms invest heavily in operating capabilities -building teams of specialists who work alongside management to identify performance bottlenecks, redesign processes, and modernize systems.

Operational excellence begins with a granular understanding of costs. Many companies lack clear visibility into their cost structures. Spending grows organically over time, budgets are built incrementally rather than from first principles, and inefficiencies accumulate. Private equity firms implement rigorous cost-analysis frameworks that illuminate opportunities for savings. They break down spending categories, challenge assumptions, and renegotiate contracts with suppliers. They introduce zero-based budgeting techniques that require managers to justify expenses rather than carry them forward automatically.

But operations extend far beyond cost. In manufacturing-heavy businesses, private equity investors focus on plant productivity, lean manufacturing practices, scrap reduction, and energy efficiency. In consumer businesses, they redesign distribution networks, improve demand forecasting, and enhance channel strategy. In service-oriented businesses, they emphasize process automation, workforce utilization, and digital tools that improve productivity. In each case, the goal is to create a more agile, more consistent, and more scalable operation.

One of the most transformative trends in recent years has been the rise of **digital value creation**. Private equity firms now employ data scientists, engineers, and digital product experts who help portfolio companies adopt modern technology. Whether through predictive analytics for demand planning, advanced pricing algorithms, digital customer acquisition funnels, or cloud migration, digital initiatives create tangible improvements in both revenues and margins. These digital transformations were once optional; today, they are essential components of the value-creation toolkit.

Governance, Leadership, and Culture: The Human Foundations of Performance

Even the most brilliant strategy and most elegant operating model will fail without strong leadership and healthy organizational culture. Private equity understands this deeply. The best firms devote considerable energy to evaluating and upgrading management teams, strengthening governance structures, and building cultures of accountability and performance.

When acquiring a company, private equity firms assess whether the existing leadership team has the capability and mindset to deliver the next phase of growth. Founders and long-tenured executives often excel at the early stages of a business but struggle with scale. In such cases, PE firms supplement or replace leadership with experienced CEOs,

CFOs, or COOs who have navigated similar growth trajectories. They introduce professional governance structures -boards with independent directors, formal decision-making processes, and clear reporting systems.

Culture is an equally important but often overlooked dimension of value creation. Many companies operate with ingrained habits that hinder performance -tolerance for mediocrity, lack of accountability, slow decision-making, or insufficient data-driven thinking. Private equity firms work to instill cultures that reward merit, embrace performance measurement, and encourage continuous improvement. By establishing clear expectations and linking incentives to outcomes, PE investors drive behavioral change that strengthens the organization over the long term.

In India, cultural transformation is particularly crucial. Many mid-sized Indian companies have historically been family-run, with informal processes and limited delegation. Bringing in structure, transparency, and professional management often unlocks latent potential. Private equity ownership accelerates this evolution, helping companies transition from promoter-driven to institutionally governed enterprises.

Capital Structure Discipline: Strengthening the Financial Engine

Another key dimension of value creation lies in optimizing the company's balance sheet. Private equity investors scrutinize capital structure with a level of rigor that many companies rarely experience. They evaluate the cost of debt, the appropriate leverage level, the maturity profile of borrowings, and the firm's interest coverage capacity. They ensure that the capital structure supports -not constrains -the company's strategy.

Capital structure optimization is not merely about adding leverage. It often involves refinancing expensive loans, negotiating better terms, diversifying lenders, and aligning financing structures with cash flow patterns. Companies sometimes underutilize debt because of risk aversion or lack of financial sophistication. In such cases, private equity firms introduce moderate leverage that improves returns while maintaining credit discipline.

Working capital management is another area where private equity creates value. Many companies tie up excessive cash in receivables or inventory. By improving credit checks, streamlining invoicing, negotiating better payment terms, and enhancing inventory forecasting, PE firms release significant cash trapped within operations. This cash can then be used for debt repayment, expansion, or shareholder distributions.

In India, where borrowing costs can be high and working capital cycles long, capital efficiency plays an especially important role. Private equity investors often bring advanced treasury practices, stronger lender relationships, and more sophisticated financial planning to optimize cash usage.

Execution and Monitoring: The Discipline That Sustains Value

A distinguishing feature of private equity ownership is the intensity of execution. Strategies are not merely articulated; they are translated into concrete action plans with clear timelines, measurable KPIs, and disciplined follow-up mechanisms. Private equity boards meet frequently -often monthly or quarterly -to evaluate progress, identify roadblocks, and recalibrate priorities. This cadence creates a sense of urgency that is often absent in public companies or family-owned businesses.

Monitoring is supported by detailed dashboards and reporting systems. Private equity firms insist on timely, accurate, and granular data. They require real-time visibility into sales performance, production efficiency, customer acquisition metrics, working capital levels, and cash flows. This transparency enhances decision-making and reduces surprises. It also fosters a culture of accountability, where managers understand that performance is continuously assessed and that course corrections are expected -not optional.

The execution discipline of private equity is one of its greatest strengths. It ensures that value creation does not remain an abstract aspiration but becomes an everyday habit embedded within the company's operations.

Exit Preparation: Engineering the Final Act of Value Creation

Every private equity investment culminates in an exit. Value creation is not complete until the company is sold, listed, or recapitalized. Preparing for exit is itself a strategic process. It involves positioning the company to command the highest possible valuation multiple from potential buyers -whether strategic acquirers, other private equity firms, or public market investors.

Exit preparation often begins years in advance. Private equity firms introduce governance structures that appeal to institutional investors, strengthen the finance function to ensure audit readiness, refine the narrative around the company's competitive advantages, and prepare detailed analyses that showcase the sustainability of improvements. They identify the most likely buyer universe and tailor the exit strategy accordingly.

In India, exit routes vary widely. Strategic sales to large corporates are common in consumer and pharmaceutical sectors. Secondary sales, where one private equity firm sells to another, are increasingly prevalent. Public listings on Indian exchanges have become more viable, particularly for companies with strong governance and stable cash flows. Private equity firms prepare meticulously for these outcomes, ensuring that the company is presented in the most compelling and transparent manner.

Value Creation in the Indian Context: Unique Challenges and Opportunities

Value creation in India carries its own distinctive characteristics. Many Indian companies have historically been promoter-driven, with informal governance and limited delegation. Decision-making is often centralized, financial reporting inconsistent, and organizational structures underdeveloped. These gaps present challenges, but they also offer immense opportunities for value creation.

Professionalizing governance is often the first step. Private equity investors help founders transition from centralized control to structured boards and empowered management teams. Introducing formal reporting lines, performance reviews, incentive structures, and succession planning often yields immediate improvements in productivity and alignment.

Operational improvements also take on a distinct flavor in India. Supply chains may be fragmented, vendor bases informal, and technology adoption uneven. Private equity firms often lead digital transformation efforts -introducing ERP systems, modernizing logistics, implementing data-driven pricing, and improving demand forecasting.

Working capital management is another area ripe for improvement. Indian companies frequently carry high levels of inventory due to supply chain unpredictability or limited analytical capabilities. They also suffer from delayed receivables, especially when dealing with distributors or institutional customers. By tightening processes and renegotiating terms, PE firms unlock substantial cash.

Finally, strategic repositioning plays a major role in India's dynamic economy. With new regulatory frameworks, evolving consumer preferences, and rapidly changing technologies, companies often need to pivot or expand into new areas. Private equity firms serve as catalysts, helping management teams explore adjacencies, launch digital extensions, or restructure legacy divisions.

Conclusion: The Art and Discipline of Creating Value

Value creation is the beating heart of private equity. It is what differentiates professional ownership from passive investment, discipline from drift, transformation from stagnation. While leverage and financial engineering can enhance returns, they cannot compensate for weak operations, flawed strategy, or poor governance. Sustainable private equity success arises from the ability to transform companies in ways that endure long after the fund exits.

This transformation is not accidental. It is the product of structured methodologies, deep expertise, rigorous analysis, and disciplined execution. It requires investors to think holistically -combining strategy, operations, finance, technology, governance, and culture into a unified value-creation blueprint. It demands empathy for the challenges companies face and decisiveness in addressing them. And it requires a commitment to long-term thinking in a world that often prizes short-term gains.

As global markets evolve and technology reshapes competition, the role of value creation in private equity will only grow more critical. In markets like India, where entrepreneurial energy is abundant but organizational maturity is still developing, the potential for private equity to create transformative impact is immense. By bringing capital, capability, and discipline together, private equity firms become instruments of economic development, corporate renewal, and enduring value.

CHAPTER 7 - DEAL SOURCING AND THE PRIVATE EQUITY INVESTMENT PROCESS

The private equity investment process is a journey of judgment, discipline, and structured reasoning. While value creation forms the heart of private equity ownership, as explored in the previous chapter, none of that is possible without the critical upstream activity of identifying and selecting the right opportunities. A private equity fund must deploy capital efficiently, intelligently, and prudently. It cannot afford to squander time or resources on companies that do not fit its strategic mandate or lack the potential to generate attractive returns. Therefore, deal sourcing and execution form the backbone of the private equity business -two interconnected processes that determine which companies enter the portfolio and which are left behind.

Despite the popular narrative of private equity firms constantly chasing deals, the reality is far more nuanced. Deal sourcing is not merely a matter of waiting for bankers to present opportunities. It is a proactive, multi-dimensional effort that blends relationship building, sector research, proprietary insights, and persistent market engagement. The best firms cultivate deep networks, develop intimate knowledge of industries, and position themselves in the minds of founders, executives, bankers, and advisors as thoughtful and value-adding partners. They do not simply react to deals; they create pathways to uncover opportunities that others may overlook.

This chapter explores the entire private equity deal sourcing and investment process -from the earliest stages of market scanning and thesis development to management meetings, diligence, valuation negotiations, investment committee approvals, deal structuring, and final signing. It paints a comprehensive narrative of how deals are born, evaluated, filtered, shaped, and ultimately consummated.

The Art and Architecture of Deal Sourcing

Deal sourcing begins long before a specific investment opportunity appears. It is rooted in a private equity firm's identity, mandate, and strategic orientation. Every fund has a particular investment philosophy -one that reflects the strengths of its partners, the guarantees made to limited partners, and its understanding of where superior returns are most likely to be found. Some firms specialize in consumer brands, others in technology, healthcare, or manufacturing. Certain firms are dedicated to buyouts, while others focus on growth equity or special situations. These preferences shape where firms search for deals and how they position themselves in the investment ecosystem.

At the heart of deal sourcing lies the cultivation of relationships. Private equity firms build long-term connections with investment bankers, boutique advisers, consultants, lawyers, auditors, and senior corporate executives. In India, this ecosystem includes global banks like Goldman Sachs or Morgan Stanley, Indian banks like Kotak and ICICI Securities, and a vast array of boutique firms that specialize in sectors such as consumer goods, healthcare, or technology. These intermediaries constantly scan the market for transaction opportunities and often serve as the first bridge between a private equity firm and a potential investment.

Yet relationships alone are not enough. They produce deal flow, but not necessarily the right kind of deal flow. The most successful firms differentiate themselves through a thesis-driven sourcing approach. Instead of reacting to whatever opportunities appear, they proactively identify themes, categories, or sub-sectors where they believe strong potential exists. These themes emerge from careful analysis of market structure, competitive dynamics, regulatory shifts, technological change, consumer trends, and macroeconomic patterns. A firm that has developed a conviction around renewable energy manufacturing, digital-first consumer brands, or contract research and manufacturing services (CRAMS) will systematically engage with companies in those verticals, develop expertise, and build credibility with founders and management teams.

This thesis-driven approach is especially powerful in India, where many attractive companies are still family-owned or not actively planning to raise capital. By demonstrating deep understanding of a sector, private equity firms can position themselves as trusted partners even before a company formally pursues funding. Over time, this creates proprietary deal flow -opportunities that come directly to the firm rather than being broadly marketed through competitive processes.

Deal sourcing also benefits from the firm's reputation. Companies prefer investors who are known for fairness, professionalism, and the ability to support long-term growth. Private equity firms that have built strong track records -by professionalizing companies, generating successful exits, and maintaining constructive relationships with founders -often see continuous inbound interest. In such cases, the firm's past performance becomes a form of intellectual magnetism, attracting opportunities without active solicitation.

From Sourcing to Screening: The First Filters

Once a potential investment opportunity is identified -whether through a banker's teaser, a founder's introduction, or proprietary outreach -the screening process begins. Screening is the act of evaluating whether the company aligns with the firm's mandate, sector expertise, deal size, geographic boundaries, and return requirements. It is a rapid assessment, designed to determine whether deeper analysis is warranted.

During screening, the investment team seeks to understand the basic architecture of the business: its revenue model, growth trajectory, unit economics, competitive position, customer concentration, management quality, and governance standards. They assess whether the company's scale and financial profile match the fund's cheque size. A firm that writes ₹500 crore equity cheques cannot spend time pursuing a ₹40 crore transaction, and a growth equity fund cannot pursue a distressed asset requiring operational repair.

The screening stage is also where initial red flags emerge. Issues related to unresolved legal disputes, opaque financial records, excessive dependence on a single customer, or conflicts between co-founders may diminish the attractiveness of the opportunity. In India, screening often involves early checks on promoter reputation, compliance history, and financial cleanliness -factors that can significantly influence diligence later.

If the company passes this initial stage, the firm typically signs a non-disclosure agreement (NDA) to access more detailed information. This marks the transition from high-level screening to deeper evaluation.

Management Meetings: Insight, Alignment, and Trust-Building

The management meeting is one of the most critical moments in the private equity investment process. It is the opportunity for the investor to understand the minds, experiences, aspirations, and integrity of the people who run the company. Private equity firms know that even the strongest business model will falter under weak leadership, while a strong leadership team can navigate unexpected adversity and uncover new opportunities.

During the first management meeting, the conversation typically begins with the company's history -how it began, how it evolved, and what challenges shaped its trajectory. Founders often recount difficult moments, pivots, or strategic choices that defined the company's survival and success. This narrative provides valuable insight into the leadership's resilience, decision-making style, and adaptability.

Private equity investors probe deeply into the company's operations. They explore the drivers of revenue growth, the composition of the customer base, the competitive landscape, the economics of the product or service, and the nature of the company's cost structure. They ask questions about margins, pricing power, capacity constraints, distribution strategies, and technological capabilities. These discussions reveal not only the company's performance but also how well management understands its own business.

Equally important is the alignment of vision. Investors assess whether the company's ambitions match the private equity firm's expectations. If the founders aspire to maintain full control while the investor requires significant influence, the partnership may not work. If founders want to pursue hypergrowth at any cost but investors prioritize disciplined expansion, strategic disagreement may ensue. The management meeting is therefore not merely an information exchange -it is the beginning of a relationship, one that requires mutual trust and alignment.

In India, cultural nuances often shape management interactions. Founders may be reluctant to disclose weaknesses, concerned about losing face or appearing vulnerable. Investors must balance rigorous questioning with empathy, patience, and an understanding of the delicate dynamics of family-run businesses. Building rapport is essential, and many successful private equity deals in India are driven as much by relationship chemistry as by financial logic.

Preliminary Analysis and the Go/No-Go Decision

After management interactions and receipt of the company's initial financial and commercial data, the investment team conducts preliminary analysis. This is a more structured and quantitative phase than screening. Here, the team constructs initial models to understand the company's financial health, growth potential, cash generation capabilities, and possible returns under different scenarios. They assess how the company compares with peers in terms of margins, pricing, and competitive positioning. They identify areas that require deeper diligence, such as customer churn, regulatory risks, environmental liabilities, or concentration exposure.

This preliminary assessment culminates in a "Go/No-Go" decision, typically discussed in an internal meeting or informally among partners. If the opportunity appears attractive and feasible, the team seeks approval to issue a non-binding term sheet or letter of intent. If the opportunity appears weak or misaligned with the fund's goals, the firm withdraws early -conserving time and resources.

The Go/No-Go stage is crucial because diligence is expensive and resource-intensive. It involves consultants, lawyers, auditors, bankers, and domain experts, all of whom need to be managed in a coordinated manner. A disciplined firm only proceeds if it has a clear hypothesis about how value will be created and an initial conviction that the deal is worth pursuing.

Due Diligence: The Search for Truth

Due diligence is the most exhaustive and rigorous phase of the investment process. It is where hypotheses are stress-tested, assumptions validated, and risks uncovered. The purpose of diligence is not merely to confirm that the company is strong -rather, it is to ensure that every material risk is understood, quantified, and priced appropriately. In private equity, surprises are costly. Diligence is the shield that protects investors from unforeseen liabilities.

This phase often spans several dimensions. Financial diligence tests the accuracy of the company's accounting, revenue recognition, cost allocations, and working capital practices. Commercial diligence examines industry trends, customer loyalty, market share stability, pricing power, and competitive threats. Legal diligence reviews contracts, compliance, litigation, and regulatory exposures. Tax diligence analyzes the structure of transactions, potential liabilities, and opportunities for optimization. Operational diligence inspects supply chains, manufacturing processes, logistics networks, and technological systems.

In recent years, technology diligence has emerged as a critical component. Investors examine the robustness of cloud infrastructure, the cybersecurity framework, the scalability of digital platforms, and the quality of software architecture. For companies in sectors like fintech, healthtech, logistics, or SaaS, such diligence is not optional -it is foundational.

In India, diligence takes on additional layers due to the complexities of promoter-driven businesses, informal practices, tax compliance variations, and evolving regulatory frameworks. Investors often scrutinize related-party transactions, land title clarity, GST compliance, ESOP documentation, and formalization of cash-based processes. The goal is not merely to identify problems but to understand whether they are manageable and whether the company's systems can evolve to meet the standards expected by institutional investors.

Diligence is also a narrative discipline. It tests whether the story the company tells -about its growth, competitiveness, and future -aligns with external realities. A founder may claim that the company is gaining market share rapidly, but customer interviews or competitor analyses may reveal a more nuanced picture. Conversely, diligence may uncover strengths the founder failed to highlight -an especially loyal customer base, superior operational processes, or hidden assets that can be leveraged for expansion.

Valuation and Deal Structuring: Translating Insights into a Transaction

Once diligence provides clarity, the firm undertakes final valuation and deal structuring. This phase combines analytical rigor with strategic negotiation. While Chapter 4 explored valuation mechanics in detail, it is important to understand valuation in the context of the investment process. Valuation is not merely a mathematical exercise; it is a negotiation shaped by emotion, expectations, competition, and the perceived quality of the asset.

Private equity firms build complex financial models that incorporate revenue forecasts, margin improvement plans, capital expenditure needs, working capital requirements, debt capacity, and potential exit scenarios. They simulate returns under various assumptions, seeking to understand how sensitive the investment is to growth, margins, exit multiples, and leverage. The firm must answer a single question with clarity: *Can this investment deliver the returns promised to investors within the risk parameters we can accept?*

Deal structuring adds another layer of sophistication. The firm negotiates equity ownership, governance rights, board representation, veto controls, liquidation preferences, anti-dilution protections, and management incentive plans. In buyouts, the firm negotiates debt terms, covenants, and repayment schedules with lenders. In minority deals, especially in India, structuring becomes even more critical because private equity firms must protect their rights without control.

The negotiation process is delicate. Founders may resist dilution, object to control provisions, or fear loss of autonomy. Private equity firms must balance firmness with respect, ensuring that negotiations do not damage trust. Deals often come together not through sheer analytical superiority, but through relationship sensitivity and the ability to align interests among all stakeholders.

Investment Committee: The Crucible of Decision-Making

The investment committee (IC) is the internal governing body where major decisions are made. It is the forum where the investment team presents their findings, defends their thesis, and seeks approval to proceed. The IC challenges assumptions, probes weaknesses, and tests whether the investment aligns with the fund's strategy and risk appetite.

An IC meeting is both analytical and philosophical. Partners debate not only the numbers but also the broader context: the company's culture, competitive durability, regulatory exposure, macroeconomic risks, and the investment team's conviction. The IC acts as the final safeguard, ensuring that emotion, momentum, or excitement do not override disciplined judgment.

If the IC approves the investment, the deal moves to documentation and closing. If not, the deal is abandoned -regardless of how much effort has been expended. This discipline is central to private equity's identity.

Documentation, Negotiation, and Closing: Converting Agreement into Reality

The final stage of the investment process involves converting the commercial agreement into legal documentation. Lawyers on both sides negotiate share purchase agreements, shareholder agreements, representations and warranties, indemnities, conditions precedent, and governance frameworks. This is a painstaking process. Every clause reflects a negotiation about risk allocation, control rights, exit mechanisms, and future behavior.

In India, documentation often requires additional steps related to regulatory filings, FDI approvals, valuation certificates, stamp duty, and compliance with sectoral guidelines. For foreign investors, frameworks such as the Foreign Exchange Management Act (FEMA) introduce additional layers of review and approval.

Closing a deal is both a legal milestone and a symbolic moment. It marks the transition from courtship to partnership. The private equity firm becomes an owner, with all the responsibilities that ownership entails. Management teams begin preparing for the post-deal integration phase, where value-creation plans come to life.

The Human Side of Dealmaking: Trust, Communication, and the Long View

Although private equity is often portrayed as a financial exercise, the investment process is ultimately human. Deals succeed not because models are perfect, but because relationships are strong, communication is transparent, and incentives are aligned. Founders and management teams must believe that the private equity firm will act as a partner, not a predator. Investors must trust that management will execute honestly and diligently.

In India, this human dimension is especially important. Many companies are built on family legacies, personal relationships, and cultural bonds. Decisions are not always purely financial; they are influenced by pride, identity, and emotional attachment. Successful private equity investors understand these nuances. They engage with humility, patience, and respect, recognizing that numbers may matter, but people matter more.

Deal Sourcing and Execution as Competitive Advantage

The best private equity firms distinguish themselves through their sourcing and execution capabilities. They know where to look, how to build trust, how to ask the right questions, how to analyze complex businesses, and how to shepherd a deal from idea to ownership. Their processes are not mechanical -they are refined through experience, intuition, and a deep understanding of the market.

In many ways, the investment process is a microcosm of the entire private equity profession. It blends strategy, finance, psychology, negotiation, and governance. It demands both analytical sharpness and emotional intelligence. And it sets the stage for what matters most: value creation, operational improvement, and delivering superior returns to investors.

CHAPTER 8 - FUNDRAISING AND PRIVATE EQUITY FUND STRUCTURES

Private equity may be defined by the deals it executes and the companies it transforms, but the industry rests upon a deeper and less visible foundation: the structure of the funds themselves. Before a private equity firm can acquire a single company, it must first raise the capital that will fuel its investment strategy. This capital does not come from retail investors or public markets. Rather, it originates from a sophisticated global network of institutional allocators -pension funds, sovereign wealth funds, endowments, insurance companies, development finance institutions, and family offices -who trust private equity firms with long durations of capital and expect disciplined stewardship, transparency, and compelling returns.

Fundraising, therefore, is not merely a preliminary requirement for private equity. It is the bedrock of the industry. A private equity firm must persuade its limited partners that it possesses a distinctive investment philosophy, a proven track record, and the organizational capabilities to deploy capital responsibly. It must convince them that its strategy aligns with their long-term objectives, risk appetite, and return requirements. And it must do all of this within a competitive environment, where hundreds of other firms are simultaneously courting the same investors.

This chapter explores how private equity firms raise capital, how they structure their funds, how they govern relationships with limited partners, and how the institutional architecture of private equity influences behavior at the fund, firm, and deal levels. It also contextualizes fundraising within the Indian landscape, where the evolution of domestic capital, regulatory frameworks, and global investor interest has shaped the emergence of one of the world's fastest-growing private equity markets.

The Origins and Purpose of Private Equity Funds

To understand fundraising, one must first understand why private equity funds exist in their modern form. Private equity is a long-duration asset class. Transforming companies takes time: years to conduct diligence, years to execute value-creation plans, years to integrate acquisitions, and years to prepare for exit. Short-term capital is incompatible with this process. Private equity requires a capital base that does not need liquidity for a decade or more, and that can tolerate periods of volatility without forcing premature exits.

The solution is a **committed capital** structure. When limited partners commit money to a private equity fund, they do not transfer all the capital immediately. Instead, they promise to supply capital whenever the general partner calls it -usually over the first four to six years. This structure ensures that the private equity firm has reliable access to capital without holding large idle cash reserves, while investors avoid paying fees on undeployed capital.

Commitment-based funds solve the liquidity mismatch that plagues most other investment structures, allowing private equity firms to make long-term decisions without fear of redemption pressure. At the same time, they impose discipline: a firm must invest only when it finds compelling opportunities. It cannot deploy capital simply because it has cash on hand, and it cannot refuse to deploy capital indefinitely without violating its commitment to limited partners.

The purpose of a private equity fund, therefore, is not merely financial. It is organizational. It creates a contractual, fiduciary relationship between a general partner and its limited partners. This relationship governs how investments are made, how returns are shared, how risks are controlled, and how the entire apparatus of private equity operates.

The General Partner and Limited Partners: Roles, Responsibilities, and Relationships

Every private equity fund exists as a partnership between the **general partner (GP)** and the **limited partners (LPs)**. The GP is the investment manager -the entity that raises capital, sources deals, conducts diligence, deploys funds, oversees portfolio companies, and executes exits. The LPs supply the capital. They delegate investment authority to the GP but retain certain rights designed to protect their interests.

The relationship between GPs and LPs is built on trust, accountability, and alignment. Alignment is crucial because the GP controls the investment process while the LP bears most of the economic risk. To ensure shared incentives, private equity compensation structures revolve around management fees, carried interest, co-investments, and GP commitments. These mechanisms ensure that the GP benefits when the LPs benefit and suffers when performance lags.

Trust is maintained through reporting and communication. LPs expect regular updates on fund performance, portfolio company developments, and market conditions. They require audited financial statements, quarterly valuations, and transparent disclosures. The GP must demonstrate discipline in deal selection, prudence in valuations, and rigor in governance. Failure to maintain LP trust can jeopardize future fundraising efforts.

The LP universe is diverse. Pension funds seek stable long-term returns to match future liabilities. Sovereign wealth funds seek diversification and global exposure. Endowments pursue high-return strategies to support institutional missions. Insurance companies invest with a focus on capital preservation and regulatory requirements. Family offices look for superior returns but value flexibility and personalized engagement. Each LP type brings unique expectations, constraints, and decision-making processes, which the GP must understand and respect.

The Fundraising Process: A Multi-Year Journey of Strategy and Persuasion

Fundraising is not an event but a campaign -one that can stretch across twelve to eighteen months, involving hundreds of meetings, presentations, and negotiations. It begins long before a fund is officially launched. Private equity firms cultivate LP relationships over decades, updating them on fund performance, sharing insights on market trends, and demonstrating consistency of strategy. When the time comes to raise a new fund, LPs should already be familiar with the firm's philosophy, track record, and capabilities.

A typical fundraising journey begins with a private equity firm evaluating its past performance and refining its investment thesis. The firm analyzes what worked well in previous funds, what challenges emerged, and how the market has changed. It then determines the size of the new fund -balancing ambition with realism, taking into account deployment pace, organizational scale, and the firm's competitive advantages.

Once the target fund size is determined, the firm prepares a private placement memorandum (PPM), a comprehensive document detailing the strategy, track record, team biographies, governance structure, fee arrangements, and risk disclosures. Alongside the PPM, the firm develops marketing materials, pitchbooks, and case studies showcasing past successes and illustrating the investment process.

The GP then embarks on a global roadshow, meeting potential LPs across financial hubs such as New York, London, Singapore, Dubai, Hong Kong, and Mumbai. These meetings are rarely straightforward. LPs conduct extensive due diligence on the GP, examining everything from historical returns to organizational culture. They analyze team stability, succession planning, investment attribution, and risk controls. They interview portfolio company CEOs, reference-check former partners, and evaluate the competitive landscape.

This due diligence phase is often as rigorous as the diligence performed by GPs on companies. LPs demand transparency on failures as well as successes. They scrutinize how the GP handled downturns, whether it exhibited discipline during market booms, and whether its valuation practices were conservative or aggressive. A GP that cannot clearly articulate its investment philosophy or attribute its returns will struggle to convince sophisticated allocators.

When LPs approve the fund, they sign limited partnership agreements (LPAs) that govern the economic and legal relationship with the GP. Once the fund reaches its closing threshold -typically after raising a majority of the target commitments -it becomes active and can begin investing.

Fund Structures: The Anatomy of a Private Equity Vehicle

Private equity funds are typically organized as closed-ended, limited partnerships. The fund has a fixed life, usually ten years, with extensions possible for two or three additional years. This structure creates a predictable timeline for capital calls, portfolio construction, value creation, exits, and capital distributions.

The life cycle of a private equity fund unfolds in distinct phases. The first phase is fundraising. Once the fund is raised, the GP enters the investment period -usually four to six years -during which it calls capital to execute new deals. After the investment period ends, the GP focuses primarily on managing and exiting existing investments. Distributions to LPs accelerate during this later phase, and by the end of the fund's life, all investments must be liquidated and proceeds returned.

The structure of incentives in private equity is also unique. Management fees, typically 1.5 to 2 percent of committed capital, provide the GP with operating income to run the organization. Carried interest -the GP's share of profits, usually around 20 percent -aligns the GP's long-term success with the LPs. Carried interest is only paid after the LPs receive their invested capital back, often with a preferred return (commonly 8 percent), creating a hurdle that incentivizes performance.

The GP also commits a portion of its own capital to the fund -usually 1 to 5 percent -to demonstrate alignment and confidence. This GP commitment can be meaningful, especially for smaller or emerging firms, and often becomes a source of pride or pressure for partners.

Fund structures often include complex mechanisms such as recycling provisions, clawbacks, catch-up clauses, and distribution waterfalls. Recycling allows the GP to reinvest early returns into new deals, increasing capital efficiency. Clawbacks ensure that if carried interest is paid prematurely due to early wins, it will be returned if later losses reduce overall fund returns. These mechanisms ensure fairness and prevent imbalance between the GP and LPs.

The Rise of Separately Managed Accounts and Co-Investments

While the traditional blind-pool fund remains the industry's backbone, LP demands have evolved. Many institutional investors now seek greater control, lower fees, and more direct exposure to individual deals. As a result, separately managed accounts (SMAs), co-investments, and customized mandates have become increasingly popular.

Co-investments allow LPs to invest directly in specific transactions alongside the GP, often with reduced or no fees. This gives LPs more granular exposure, enables faster capital deployment, and strengthens relationships with the GP. For the GP, co-investments help finance larger deals without over-concentrating the fund and create stronger alignment with key LPs.

Separately managed accounts give an LP exclusive access to a tailored portfolio managed by the GP. These accounts require sophisticated infrastructure and deep trust but offer more flexibility in terms of fees, strategy, and governance.

These innovations reflect the growing maturity of the private equity ecosystem. As the asset class expands, LPs seek more influence and customization, while GPs diversify their sources of fee income.

The Indian Fundraising Landscape: Challenges, Evolution, and the Rise of Domestic Capital

India's private equity fundraising landscape has undergone a dramatic transformation over the last two decades. In the early 2000s, global investors viewed India as an emerging frontier market -interesting, but fraught with risk, limited governance, and underdeveloped liquidity pathways. Fundraising was slow and dependent on global cycles.

Over time, as India liberalized sectors, strengthened regulatory frameworks, and delivered successful exits, confidence grew. Global LPs increasingly recognized India as one of the most attractive long-term investment destinations, driven by demographic tailwinds, rising consumption, and entrepreneurial dynamism. Firms such as ChrysCapital, True North, Multiples, Kedaara, and Premji Invest established deep relationships with global LPs, showcasing the returns possible in India.

Today, fundraising for India-focused funds remains competitive but far more stable and diversified. Sovereign wealth funds and pension funds from Canada, Singapore, and the Middle East have become significant contributors. Development finance institutions continue to support first-time managers and strategies aligned with national priorities such as healthcare, financial inclusion, and renewable energy.

Perhaps the most important shift has been the rise of **domestic Indian capital**. Insurance companies, family offices, corporate treasuries, and high-net-worth individuals have begun allocating more meaningfully to private equity and venture capital. Regulatory changes allowing domestic institutions to invest a portion of their assets in alternative funds have opened new channels of fundraising. This emergence of domestic LPs enhances the resilience of the Indian private market and reduces dependence on global liquidity cycles.

Challenges remain. Domestic LP sophistication is still developing, regulatory frameworks evolve continuously, and global macroeconomic volatility impacts fundraising cycles. Yet the long-term trajectory is clear: India is moving toward a balanced mix of global and domestic capital, strengthening the foundation for sustained growth in private equity activity.

Governance, Transparency, and the Institutionalization of the Asset Class

As private equity has become a central pillar of global capital allocation, LP expectations have grown more sophisticated. Transparency, discipline, and governance are now non-negotiable. GPs must provide detailed reporting, adhere to valuation standards, and maintain robust internal controls. LPs expect clarity on portfolio construction, risk management, ESG performance, and compliance systems.

Environmental, social, and governance (ESG) considerations, once peripheral, have become mainstream. Many LPs, especially sovereign wealth funds and pension funds, require GPs to demonstrate ESG integration into investment processes. This includes climate risk assessment, diversity initiatives, data privacy protections, and responsible governance frameworks. ESG is no longer a marketing tool; it is an investment requirement that shapes fundraising success.

The institutionalization of private equity also means increased competition. LPs have more choices than ever -across strategies, geographies, and fund structures. GPs must differentiate themselves through performance, expertise, thought leadership, sector specialization, and transparency. The era of easy fundraising is over; only firms that demonstrate excellence in all aspects of the investment and organizational lifecycle will consistently attract capital.

The Interplay Between Fund Structure and Investment Behavior

The structure of private equity funds influences investment behavior in profound ways. The need to deploy capital within the investment period creates a balance between discipline and urgency. GPs must avoid both under-investment, which can lead to subscale funds, and over-aggressive deployment, which increases risk. The fixed life of the fund encourages active management and structured exits, preventing indefinite ownership.

The incentive structure, particularly carried interest, promotes entrepreneurial behavior within the GP. Partners are motivated to generate superior returns, strengthen deal quality, and execute value-creation plans. At times, these incentives may create tension between short-term optimization and long-term sustainability, which is why LP oversight and governance mechanisms are essential.

Recycling provisions allow funds to reinvest early proceeds, enhancing flexibility but requiring discipline. Clawback rules protect LPs, ensuring fairness in profit-sharing. All of these features shape the culture, priorities, and rhythms of the GP's work.

In India, fund structures have become increasingly sophisticated. Hybrid vehicles, evergreen structures, and multi-strategy platforms have emerged, reflecting the breadth of opportunities and the diversity of investor needs. Domestic LP participation has encouraged innovation in fund terms and governance, aligning structures more closely with Indian market realities.

Conclusion: The Architecture Beneath the Enterprise of Private Equity

Fundraising and fund structures form the institutional scaffolding that supports the private equity industry. Without committed capital, aligned incentives, rigorous governance, and long-term LP relationships, the entire system would collapse. The deals, the value creation, the exits -everything rests on this foundation.

The GP-LP relationship is built on trust, performance, and mutual commitment. It is a partnership that spans decades, cycles, and strategic evolutions. Private equity firms must not only deploy capital effectively but also steward relationships, uphold fiduciary duties, maintain transparency, and adapt to a rapidly changing world. Meanwhile, LPs must evaluate GPs with sophistication, patience, and discernment.

As the industry matures globally and in India, fundraising becomes both more challenging and more strategically significant. Competition for capital intensifies, LP expectations rise, and the need for differentiation grows. Yet at the same time, opportunities expand. Institutional capital seeks long-term, uncorrelated returns, and private equity offers precisely that. With strong governance, disciplined execution, and clear investment philosophy, private equity firms can build enduring relationships with LPs and secure the capital required to pursue transformative investments.

Fund structures shape behavior, incentives, and decision-making. They create the time horizon that enables long-term value creation and establish the guardrails that govern risk. In understanding these structures, one gains insight not only into the mechanics of private equity but into the philosophy of stewardship that underlies it.

In the end, fundraising is more than the gathering of capital. It is the creation of a covenant between investors and managers -a shared belief in the ability of private equity, executed with discipline and wisdom, to transform companies, create wealth, and contribute to the global economy.

CHAPTER 9 - DUE DILIGENCE IN PRIVATE EQUITY

Due diligence is the investigative engine of private equity. It is the systematic, deeply analytical process by which an investment thesis transitions from possibility into conviction. While deal sourcing identifies opportunities and valuation quantifies them, due diligence validates whether those opportunities are truly viable and whether those valuations stand on solid foundations. It is, in many respects, the most intellectually demanding and multidimensional element of private equity investing. A successful due diligence process uncovers the inner workings of a company -not only what is visible in financial statements, but also the implicit assumptions, cultural patterns, operational intricacies, competitive dynamics, and external risks that shape the company's future.

To those outside the industry, due diligence may appear to be a mechanical verification exercise -a compliance step consisting of cross-checking numbers and validating documents. In reality, it is far more profound and interpretive. Due diligence seeks to answer a fundamental question: *Is the company truly what it appears to be, and can it become what we believe it can become?* This question cannot be answered by numbers alone; it requires disciplined inquiry, contextual understanding, and a holistic view of the business. The due diligence process blends finance, analytics, strategy, psychology, law, operations, and risk management into a unified framework aimed at uncovering truth.

The stakes of diligence are high. A single overlooked weakness -a customer concentration issue, a misreported margin, a regulatory liability, a flawed technology stack, or a cultural dysfunction -can derail an investment and destroy years of value creation. Conversely, strong diligence can reveal hidden strengths, uncover neglected opportunities, and strengthen an investor's conviction in a company's potential. The purpose of diligence is therefore not only protective but also constructive. It clarifies where value resides and how it can be amplified.

This chapter explores the philosophy, structure, and execution of due diligence in private equity from a narrative, descriptive perspective. It examines the major dimensions of diligence -financial, commercial, operational, legal, tax, technology, and ESG -while weaving together insights on how investors analyze companies holistically. It also explores the unique challenges and nuances of diligence in the Indian market, where informal practices, regulatory complexities, and rapid growth can complicate the search for truth.

The Purpose of Due Diligence: From Curiosity to Conviction

At its core, due diligence is an exercise in intellectual honesty. It forces investors to confront the assumptions embedded in their investment thesis and to validate them with evidence. Private equity investing begins with narrative -an idea about how a company can grow, transform, or reposition itself. But narrative, no matter how compelling, must be tested against reality. Diligence is the bridge between imagination and discipline. It takes the investor's initial excitement and subjects it to sceptical, forensic analysis.

The purpose of diligence is not to eliminate risk; private equity investing by its nature involves uncertainty. Rather, diligence seeks to eliminate *unknown* risk -the type that emerges after an investment is made and cannot be priced or controlled. Known risks can be managed, negotiated, or mitigated. Unknown risks create blind spots that threaten returns.

Diligence is also about understanding how value will be created. A financial model may forecast margin improvements, market share gains, or working capital efficiencies. But diligence must determine whether these forecasts are realistic. Can the company realistically raise prices without losing customers? Is the TAM (total addressable market) truly as large as management claims? Are competitors weaker than they appear, or are they poised to outpace the company? Is the technology architecture robust enough to support scale? These are not theoretical questions. They are the foundation of investment conviction.

In practice, due diligence is a dialogue between optimism and scepticism. The investment team must maintain enthusiasm for the opportunity while subjecting every assumption to relentless scrutiny. The best private equity investors are those who remain intellectually flexible -willing to refine or even abandon their thesis as new information emerges. Diligence is thus not a validation process; it is a learning process.

Financial Due Diligence: Interpreting the Numbers Behind the Narrative

Financial due diligence is often the first-dimension investors explore. It examines the historical financial statements of the company -its revenue patterns, margins, cost structures, working capital cycles, capital expenditure requirements, and cash flow profiles. But true financial diligence is not merely a review of numbers; it is an investigation into the *economic engine* of the business.

The purpose of financial diligence is to understand the economic reality that financial statements represent. The numbers must reflect consistent accounting policies, clean reporting, and genuine business performance -not window dressing or selective disclosure. Investors examine whether revenue recognition policies are conservative or aggressive, whether cost allocations are transparent or manipulated, and whether the company's reported EBITDA reflects actual cash profitability or masks structural inefficiencies.

Patterns matter immensely. A company that has grown revenue quickly but without corresponding improvements in contribution margin may be expanding inefficiently. A business that shows strong EBITDA but weak cash flow may be capital intensive or suffering from poor receivable collection. A company with attractive margins in aggregate may look less compelling when margins are analyzed by geography, product line, or customer segment.

Working capital diligence is often where the deepest insights emerge. Many businesses, especially in India, exhibit significant working capital imbalances -slow collections, extended credit terms, excessive inventory, or poorly negotiated supplier contracts. These dynamics can reveal vulnerabilities that affect cash flow, debt capacity, and valuation. Private equity investors explore whether working capital can be improved through better processes, stronger management oversight, or renegotiated terms.

Historical financials also serve as a basis for forecasting. Investors must determine whether past trends are indicative of future performance or distorted by one-off events, exceptional items, or legacy contracts. In India, for instance, revenue spikes sometimes occur around year-end due to channel stuffing or aggressive booking practices. Diligence must uncover whether revenue quality is consistent, repeatable, and aligned with customer behavior.

Ultimately, financial diligence provides a foundation for valuation. If financial statements are unreliable or inflated, the valuation becomes meaningless. A disciplined investor uses financial diligence to establish an accurate baseline from which all value creation planning can proceed.

Commercial Due Diligence: Understanding Markets, Customers, and Competitors

Commercial due diligence investigates the external environment in which the company operates. It examines the size of the market, the pace of its growth, the competitive landscape, customer loyalty, pricing dynamics, and macroeconomic factors that may shape demand. In many ways, commercial diligence is a test of whether the company's growth narrative is grounded in market reality.

The heart of commercial diligence lies in understanding the company's position within its industry. Investors analyze whether the company is a market leader, a challenger, a niche player, or a vulnerable incumbent. Each position carries different risks and opportunities. Market leaders may enjoy economies of scale and brand strength but attract regulatory or competitive pressure. Challengers may have high growth potential but require significant investment to capture share. Niche players may be defensible but lack scalability.

Customer interviews serve as one of the most powerful tools in commercial diligence. They reveal how customers perceive the company's products or services, what alternatives they consider, how price-sensitive they are, and why they stay or churn. These conversations provide insights that no financial statement can offer. They reveal whether the company's value proposition is truly differentiated or merely adequate. They uncover whether customers view the company as a strategic partner or a transactional vendor subject to replacement.

Competitive analysis adds another dimension. Private equity investors study existing competitors, emerging disruptors, and adjacent industries that could pose threats. They analyze competitor pricing, customer acquisition strategies, supply chain structures, and capital investment patterns. They examine whether new entrants face high barriers or whether the industry is ripe for technological disruption.

Market growth is another critical factor. A strong company in a shrinking market may struggle to sustain performance, while a mediocre company in a rapidly expanding market may appear stronger than it truly is. Investors examine long-term demographic trends, regulatory developments, technological enablers, and shifts in consumer preferences that influence the company's growth trajectory.

In India, commercial diligence often involves understanding unique market structures. Fragmented supply chains, informal distribution channels, regional preferences, and heterogeneous consumer behavior complicate market assessment. A pan-India consumer brand may be strong in southern states but weak in the north. A logistics company may face widely varying competitive dynamics between metro and tier-2 cities. Commercial diligence must capture these nuances with specificity and accuracy.

Operational Due Diligence: Examining the Engines of Execution

While commercial diligence analyzes the market, operational diligence examines the company's ability to execute within that market. It focuses on the systems, processes, infrastructure, and capabilities that allow a company to deliver its products or services efficiently and reliably.

Operational diligence often reveals gaps that can significantly affect value creation. A company may have strong revenue growth but weak operational controls. It may have excellent products but inefficient manufacturing. It may operate in a high-growth sector but suffer from supply chain bottlenecks. Private equity investors investigate these operational bottlenecks with the same intensity that engineers might apply when diagnosing machinery.

Manufacturing businesses require analysis of plant efficiency, production scheduling, maintenance practices, scrap rates, and energy utilization. Service businesses require evaluation of workforce productivity, process automation, service-level adherence, and quality controls. Consumer businesses demand assessment of distribution networks, channel economics, and retail execution.

Technology often becomes a focal point. Many companies operate with legacy systems that inhibit scalability, transparency, or efficiency. ERP systems may be outdated or poorly integrated. Data may be fragmented across departments. Cybersecurity measures may be insufficient. Private equity investors evaluate whether the company's technology infrastructure supports its growth ambitions or whether substantial upgrades will be required.

In India, operational diligence frequently uncovers gaps resulting from informal practices, manual processes, and limited investment in systems. A company might rely on spreadsheets instead of ERP systems, or maintain handwritten records for inventory management. These gaps represent both risks and opportunities. While they pose short-term challenges, they also offer substantial value creation potential if addressed effectively.

Legal and Regulatory Due Diligence: Navigating Risks and Obligations

Legal due diligence examines the company's contractual, regulatory, and compliance landscape. It seeks to identify liabilities, breaches, disputes, and risks that could undermine the investment. In markets like India, where regulatory frameworks are complex, evolving, and sometimes inconsistently applied, legal diligence is especially important.

Private equity investors examine customer and vendor contracts to assess terms, obligations, renewal structures, exclusivity clauses, pricing adjustments, and termination rights. They review shareholder agreements, joint venture documents, intellectual property ownership, employment contracts, and litigation history. They evaluate land titles, environmental permits, and statutory compliances.

Regulatory diligence is particularly crucial in sectors such as healthcare, financial services, education, infrastructure, and telecommunications, where licenses, approvals, and compliance frameworks shape the viability of the business. A healthcare provider may face stringent clinical compliance requirements. A financial services company must comply with RBI, SEBI, or IRDAI regulations. A renewable energy business may be affected by state-level policies.

Legal diligence aims to reveal whether the company maintains a culture of compliance or whether it operates with informal shortcuts. This analysis often shapes the negotiation of representations, warranties, indemnities, and escrow arrangements in transaction documents.

Tax Due Diligence: Understanding Obligations, Liabilities, and Opportunities

Tax diligence assesses the company's historic tax compliance, potential liabilities, and the tax implications of the proposed transaction. Investors analyze whether the company has adhered to GST, TDS, transfer pricing, MAT, and corporate tax regulations. They examine whether tax planning practices are conservative or aggressive.

Tax diligence also informs deal structuring. The choice of jurisdiction, the design of share purchase agreements, the use of special purpose vehicles, and the structuring of promoter payouts must all reflect tax efficiency, legality, and long-term feasibility. Indian tax laws have evolved rapidly, and private equity firms must ensure that the transaction structure minimizes risk of retrospective liabilities.

Technology and Cyber Due Diligence: Evaluating the Digital Backbone

As businesses become increasingly technology-driven, technology diligence has moved from optional to indispensable. Investors analyze whether the company's technology stack can support growth, whether data protection protocols are robust, whether the architecture is scalable, and whether cybersecurity safeguards are adequate.

This analysis is critical not only for SaaS or fintech companies but also for traditional businesses. Manufacturers require IoT-enabled systems for predictive maintenance. Retailers need robust ERP and CRM systems. Logistics companies depend on real-time tracking and optimization algorithms. Without a stable technology backbone, growth initiatives may falter.

Cyber risk has become a central concern. Breaches, ransomware attacks, and data leaks can destroy value, damage reputation, and trigger regulatory penalties. Investors evaluate access controls, encryption practices, incident response plans, and cyber maturity levels.

Environmental, Social, and Governance (ESG) Diligence: The Emerging Imperative

ESG diligence has become mainstream. It evaluates how the company manages environmental impact, labor practices, governance standards, and stakeholder relationships. Investors analyze sustainability reports, energy usage, emissions levels, waste management, employee welfare, workplace safety, board independence, diversity policies, and ethical practices.

In India, ESG diligence often reveals deficiencies in environmental compliance, labor documentation, safety systems, and governance transparency. Private equity investors increasingly integrate ESG improvements into value creation plans, recognizing that responsible behavior reduces risk and enhances long-term equity value.

Synthesizing Insights: Building the Integrated Diligence View

One of the most intellectually challenging aspects of due diligence is synthesizing findings across disciplines. Commercial strength may be offset by operational weakness. Financial robustness may be undermined by legal uncertainty. A strong technology platform may be constrained by weak governance. Investors must integrate dozens of insights into a coherent analytical view that informs valuation, deal structure, and negotiation strategy.

The synthesis process involves collaboration across internal teams, external consultants, and subject matter experts. It requires humility -recognizing when a thesis must be revised -and judgment -determining which risks are acceptable and which cannot be tolerated. It demands that the investment team balance risk mitigation with opportunity evaluation, neither overstating minor weaknesses nor overlooking major structural issues.

Due Diligence in India: Complexity, Informality, and Hidden Opportunity

Due diligence in India carries distinctive challenges. Informal business practices, fragmented markets, evolving regulations, and inconsistent financial reporting complicate the diligence process. Yet these same complexities create opportunities. A company with inconsistent financial records may nonetheless possess strong operational capabilities. A company with informal processes may improve dramatically under institutional ownership. The purpose of diligence in

India is not to find perfect businesses; it is to find businesses capable of becoming outstanding under the right stewardship.

Indian diligence often requires deeper triangulation than in Western markets. Investors rely not only on documents but also on-site visits, customer interviews, supplier checks, competitive intelligence, and local market insights. Informal payments, land title ambiguities, and historical tax issues require nuanced understanding rather than blanket rejection.

The Indian diligence landscape has also matured. As more companies professionalize and more investors enter the market, the quality of data, governance, and reporting has improved significantly. However, the diligence process remains more investigative and interpretive than in developed markets, requiring both local expertise and international discipline.

Conclusion: The Discipline That Anchors Private Equity

Due diligence is the bedrock of private equity discipline. It ensures that investment decisions are grounded in reality, that risks are understood, and that opportunities are validated. It transforms enthusiasm into conviction, narrative into evidence, and possibility into strategy. Through diligence, private equity investors come to understand not only whether a company is worth investing in, but *how* to invest, *where* to create value, and *what* the journey ahead will require.

Diligence is ultimately an act of stewardship. It reflects the investor's responsibility to their limited partners, to the management teams they will work with, and to the companies they will help transform. It demands rigor, humility, curiosity, and judgment. It is both a science and an art -structured yet interpretive, analytical yet intuitive.

As private equity continues to evolve in India and around the world, the importance of robust diligence will only grow. Markets become more competitive, valuations rise, and risks multiply. In such an environment, the ability to uncover truth -to see a company clearly, in all its strengths and weaknesses -is the greatest advantage an investor can possess. Due diligence is not a back-office procedure; it is the gateway to excellence in private equity investing.

CHAPTER 10 - PORTFOLIO MANAGEMENT AND MONITORING IN PRIVATE EQUITY

If deal sourcing is the courtship and due diligence the engagement, portfolio management is the marriage -the long period during which the private equity firm works hand-in-hand with management to build a stronger, more profitable, more resilient company. Yet for all the attention given to fundraising, dealmaking, and valuation, it is portfolio management that ultimately distinguishes exceptional private equity firms from average ones. This is where value is created, sustained, and realized. It is where strategy becomes execution, conviction becomes results, and ownership becomes transformation.

Portfolio management is not a single discipline but an ecosystem of activities -strategic guidance, operational improvement, governance oversight, financial optimization, leadership development, risk management, and digital transformation -all executed under the pressure of time and the expectation of generating superior returns. It requires a delicate balance of influence and restraint, intuition and analysis, long-term planning and short-term action. The nature of private equity ownership imposes urgency: the clock starts ticking the moment a deal is signed, and every month lost is a month that cannot be recovered by the time of exit.

This chapter explores the philosophy, practice, and challenges of portfolio management in private equity. It paints a holistic picture of how private equity firms work with management teams, deploy operating expertise, monitor performance, navigate crises, and position companies for successful exit. It also contextualizes these practices within the Indian environment, where promoter dynamics, governance norms, and market structures influence how portfolio oversight must be conducted.

The Transition from Deal to Ownership: Establishing the Foundation

The moment the deal closes, the private equity investment transforms from a theoretical model into a living enterprise with thousands of moving parts. The transition from diligence mode to ownership mode is both delicate and decisive. During diligence, the investor is an outsider -probing, questioning, evaluating. After closing, the investor becomes an insider -owner, partner, and steward. This shift requires recalibrating the relationship with management, resetting expectations, and building trust that will last years.

Private equity firms typically begin with a hundred-day plan -a structured set of priorities designed to create momentum, clarify governance, and stabilize the organization. But more importantly, they initiate a deeper dialogue with the CEO and leadership team to understand the cultural tone of the organization, the motivations of key managers, and the unspoken dynamics that shape decision-making.

Every portfolio company is unique. Some require immediate intervention -cost realignment, leadership changes, refinancing, or operational restructuring. Others require restraint, allowing management the space and confidence to continue executing. The art of portfolio management lies in discerning which approach to adopt. Too much interference risks demoralizing the management team and stifling initiative; too little risks inertia and missed opportunities.

In India, the initial transition often involves aligning with promoters or founders who may retain ownership stakes or operational roles. Navigating this dynamic requires sensitivity. Founders typically possess deep domain knowledge, emotional attachment to the business, and strong personal networks. Private equity firms must balance the need for professionalization with respect for the founder's legacy, ensuring collaboration rather than conflict.

Governance as the First Pillar of Portfolio Management

Governance is the architecture through which private equity firms oversee their companies. The board becomes the primary forum for strategic direction, performance review, and decision-making. A well-functioning board establishes clarity of roles, accountability of executives, and discipline in execution.

Upon acquisition, private equity firms often reshape the board's composition. They may introduce independent directors with sector expertise, financial acumen, or operational experience. They may streamline the board's structure to ensure agility and efficiency. They often reform reporting processes, establish audit and risk committees, and embed governance practices aligned with institutional standards.

Governance is not bureaucratic oversight; it is a mechanism for ensuring that management decisions are grounded in facts, aligned with strategy, and subject to informed debate. Board meetings become high-stakes conversations where assumptions are challenged, alternatives evaluated, and risks surfaced. Private equity firms encourage transparency, discouraging optimistic narratives unsupported by data.

In founder-led companies, governance enhancement is often transformative. Many Indian businesses historically operated with informal reporting, minimal delegation, and decision-making concentrated in the hands of a single individual. Private equity firms help institutionalize processes, introduce data-driven reviews, and create systems that reduce dependence on individuals. Although this transition can be culturally challenging, it lays the foundation for scalable and resilient growth.

Strategic Oversight: Reaffirming, Refining, and Reinventing the Business

Portfolio management requires continual engagement with strategy. Even the most compelling acquisition thesis must evolve as markets shift, competitors adapt, and internal capabilities change. Private equity firms remain deeply involved in shaping strategy, although execution remains the responsibility of management.

Sometimes, the strategy envisioned during diligence remains intact. In other cases, diligence uncovers opportunities that only crystallize after ownership begins. Private equity firms push companies to revisit fundamental questions: What business are we really in? Which segments offer sustainable growth? Where are we vulnerable? What should we stop doing? What capabilities must we build?

Strategic oversight often involves deciding whether the company should expand into adjacencies, enter new geographies, invest in technology, reposition its brand, or diversify its product portfolio. It may require bold decisions -exiting legacy businesses, shutting down loss-making units, or reshaping the organizational structure.

In India, strategic realignment often involves shifting from informal, opportunistic growth to disciplined, structured expansion. Many Indian companies operate in multiple segments, sometimes as a result of historical curiosity or opportunism. Private equity firms help sharpen focus -prioritizing the segments that offer the greatest returns and shedding those that distract from core strengths.

Operational Excellence: Turning Vision into Performance

Operational improvement is the engine room of private equity ownership. While strategy identifies "what" needs to be achieved, operations determine "how" it will be accomplished. Private equity firms deploy operating partners -experts in supply chain, pricing, manufacturing, finance, sales, and digital transformation -to work alongside management teams.

These operating partners are not consultants in the traditional sense. They act as collaborators, coaches, and catalysts within the company. They embed themselves in operations, identify inefficiencies, co-create improvement plans, and help implement changes. Their tenure -typically aligned with the full investment lifecycle -gives them far deeper impact than short-term advisors.

Operational excellence manifests differently depending on the company's nature. In a consumer company, it may involve optimizing trade promotions, refining channel strategies, or enhancing demand forecasting. In a manufacturing company, it may require improving plant utilization, implementing lean practices, or modernizing equipment. In services businesses, it may focus on workforce productivity, process automation, and customer experience.

Technology has become a central pillar of operational improvement. Private equity firms push portfolio companies to adopt digital tools -ERP upgrades, CRM systems, pricing analytics, digital marketing, predictive maintenance, automation platforms, and data warehouses. These transformations, once optional, now shape competitive advantage.

In India, operational excellence takes on additional complexity. Supply chains may be informal, distribution fragmented, and processes manual. Introducing discipline into such environments demands patience, adaptability, and strong change management. Yet the upside is enormous: Indian companies often show dramatic performance improvements once operational rigor is implemented.

Financial Management: Strengthening the Balance Sheet and Fuelling Growth

Private equity ownership brings a heightened emphasis on financial discipline. Companies must manage cash with precision, maintain efficient working capital cycles, and allocate capital wisely. Financial management becomes a shared responsibility between the CFO, management team, and the private equity firm.

The CFO's role is often elevated under private equity ownership. Many firms replace or strengthen the finance leadership early in the ownership period. Investors expect real-time reporting, robust forecasting, reliable budgeting, and strong controls. They push for clarity on revenue drivers, cost dynamics, and capital requirements.

Working capital management is especially important in India. Many companies suffer from slow receivables, excess inventory, and inconsistent cash discipline. Private equity firms introduce dashboards, policy changes, and process improvements that unlock cash and strengthen liquidity.

Capital allocation becomes more analytical. Investment decisions are evaluated through rigorous hurdle rates and return analyses. Capex must demonstrate clear payback potential. Acquisitions undergo strategic and financial filtering before approval. This discipline ensures that scarce capital flows to the initiatives with the highest returns.

In leveraged buyouts, debt management becomes central. Investors monitor covenant compliance, refinancing cycles, and interest coverage. They ensure that the company does not breach covenants that could trigger penalties or lender intervention. Even in growth equity deals, where leverage is modest, financial discipline enhances resilience and reduces risk.

Leadership and Talent: The Human Lever of Value Creation

No amount of strategy or operational improvement can succeed without the right leadership. Private equity firms place enormous emphasis on people -evaluating whether the CEO, CFO, COO, and broader management team possess the capabilities, temperament, and alignment required to execute the value-creation plan.

Leadership assessments often begin immediately after closing. Investors evaluate whether the CEO is suited for the next stage of growth. A founder who excelled at entrepreneurial hustle may struggle with the structured discipline required for scaling. A seasoned corporate executive may lack the agility needed for a fast-growing business.

Talent gaps sometimes appear quickly. Private equity firms may need to recruit new leaders -bringing in a professional CFO, a head of operations, a CHRO, or a chief technology officer. The talent upgrade may extend deeper into the organization, reshaping sales teams, engineering teams, or plant management.

The CHRO's role becomes increasingly central. Private equity investors recognize that culture determines execution. A culture that avoids accountability, tolerates mediocrity, or resists change can undermine transformation. Investors work with CHROs to implement performance management systems, incentive structures, succession planning, and employee engagement initiatives.

In India, talent transitions require sensitivity. Founders may view leadership changes as threats. Employees may resist new structures. Investors must navigate these dynamics with patience, ensuring that professionalization does not alienate key contributors or destabilize the organization.

Monitoring and Reporting: The Rhythm of Private Equity Ownership

Portfolio monitoring is the structured process through which private equity firms track performance, identify risks, and ensure accountability. It is characterized by rigorous reporting, monthly dashboards, key performance indicators, and frequent interactions with management.

Unlike public investors, private equity firms do not rely on quarterly earnings calls. They maintain continuous visibility into the company's operations. They receive weekly or monthly reports detailing revenue, margins, production metrics, sales funnel data, working capital cycles, cash balances, and progress against value-creation initiatives.

Board meetings become focal points for monitoring. They provide forums for reviewing performance trends, debating strategic choices, and making operational decisions. Discussions are candid, analytical, and forward-looking. Investors challenge assumptions, request clarity, and encourage course corrections when necessary.

Monitoring is not about micromanagement; it is about discipline. It ensures that the value-creation blueprint remains alive, adaptable, and measurable. It prevents drift, inertia, or complacency. It fosters a culture in which decisions are made based on evidence rather than intuition alone.

In India, monitoring plays an even more important role due to the prevalence of informal processes. Regular reporting helps institutionalize discipline and align cross-functional teams. It also builds visibility into the complexities of India's regulatory, tax, and market environment.

Crisis Management: Navigating Shocks with Agility and Resolve

No investment sails smoothly for its entire duration. Companies face unforeseen challenges -market downturns, regulatory shifts, supply chain disruptions, leadership departures, technology failures, customer losses, and macroeconomic volatility. Private equity firms must be prepared to guide their portfolio companies through crises with agility and clarity.

When crises emerge, private equity firms often operate in "war-room mode." They conduct rapid diagnostic assessments, assemble cross-functional task forces, implement cash preservation measures, and engage deeply with management. They support communication with lenders, customers, employees, and regulators. They make swift decisions -sometimes replacing leaders, restructuring operations, or pivoting strategies.

The COVID-19 pandemic exemplified the importance of strong crisis management. Private equity firms across India mobilized resources to stabilize supply chains, support remote working, renegotiate contracts, and preserve liquidity. Many firms emerged from the crisis stronger, with heightened operational resilience and deeper trust between investors and management.

Crisis moments often reveal the true strength of the investor-management partnership. Firms that have built trust, transparency, and disciplined processes manage crises more effectively than those that relied solely on financial engineering.

Driving Digital Transformation: A Modern Imperative

In recent years, digital transformation has become a core component of portfolio management. Investors increasingly view technology as a critical driver of competitive advantage, efficiency, and scalability. Digital initiatives span a wide spectrum -from ERP modernization to advanced analytics, digital marketing, customer experience platforms, automation, and AI-driven optimization.

Private equity firms deploy digital experts who assess the company's technological maturity, identify gaps, and develop transformation roadmaps. These roadmaps integrate technology investments with broader strategic goals. A logistics company might invest in route optimization algorithms. A consumer company may embrace omnichannel engagement. A manufacturing company may implement IoT sensors for predictive maintenance.

In India, digital adoption is particularly powerful due to the country's ecosystem of affordable cloud solutions, digital infrastructure, and rapidly evolving customer expectations. Companies that embrace digital transformation often leapfrog competitors, enhancing revenue growth and operational efficiency.

ESG Integration: Building Sustainable and Responsible Companies

Environmental, social, and governance (ESG) considerations have become essential in portfolio management. Investors assess environmental impact, energy usage, labor practices, diversity, safety standards, and governance transparency. They integrate ESG goals into value-creation plans -seeking not only compliance but proactive improvements.

Indian companies often require substantial ESG strengthening. Private equity firms help establish safety protocols, formalize labor documentation, implement environmental controls, and introduce ethical governance practices. These initiatives reduce risks, enhance brand reputation, and attract institutional investors at exit.

Preparing for Exit: Shaping the Final Chapter

Portfolio management culminates in exit preparation. As the investment horizon approaches maturity, private equity firms shift focus from transformation to positioning. They refine the company's narrative, strengthen financial controls, finalize leadership transitions, benchmark valuations, and prepare detailed analyses for potential buyers.

Exit options include strategic sales, secondary sales, IPOs, or promoter buybacks. Each option requires distinct preparation. Strategic buyers seek synergy narratives. Public markets demand stable governance and predictable performance. Secondary buyers require evidence of continued upside.

Private equity firms guide management through these preparations with precision. They ensure that the company presents itself in the most compelling manner, with clear performance metrics, defensible forecasts, and validated value-creation achievements.

In India, exit timing requires sensitivity to macroeconomic cycles, sector sentiment, and regulatory environments. Investors may hold assets longer to maximize value or expedite exits when market windows open.

Conclusion: The Stewardship That Defines Private Equity

Portfolio management is the essence of private equity. It is the disciplined, relentless, collaborative effort through which investors turn companies into better versions of themselves. It blends strategy, operations, finance, governance, leadership, culture, digital transformation, and crisis navigation. It requires patience, courage, humility, and expertise.

A private equity firm's reputation is shaped not by how many deals it executes but by how well it manages the companies it owns. Great firms create lasting value that endures long after they exit. They turn fragmented businesses into national champions, family-run enterprises into institutional powerhouses, and good companies into exceptional ones.

In India, portfolio management is especially transformative. It brings structure to informal environments, discipline to evolving markets, and professionalization to generational businesses. It accelerates growth, modernizes operations, and fosters long-term competitiveness.

When done well, portfolio management becomes a profound act of stewardship -one that benefits not only investors, but employees, customers, suppliers, communities, and the broader economy. It is the heart of private equity's promise: that disciplined ownership can build stronger companies and create enduring value.

CHAPTER 11 - EXIT STRATEGIES IN PRIVATE EQUITY

Exiting an investment is the defining moment of the private equity journey. It is the culmination of years of effort -deal sourcing, conviction building, value creation, governance strengthening, financial discipline, operational improvement, and strategic repositioning. Everything the private equity firm has done since the day it acquired the company ultimately converges on the exit. A successful exit validates the original thesis, rewards limited partners, strengthens the firm's reputation, and creates momentum for future fundraising. A weak exit, by contrast, can overshadow years of hard work and raise uncomfortable questions about judgment, timing, and execution.

Exits are far more than transactional events. They require deep strategy, market intelligence, emotional intelligence, and precise timing. They must reflect both the company's readiness and the market's receptivity. They demand storytelling -the ability to articulate not just what the company is, but what it has become under private equity ownership and what it can continue to become under new ownership. They require orchestration, as dozens of stakeholders -management teams, bankers, lawyers, auditors, buyers, regulators, and the private equity firm itself -must align around a common objective. And they require discipline, because the temptation to exit too early or too late is ever-present, influenced by market cycles, sector sentiment, and internal fund dynamics.

This chapter explores the full breadth of exit strategies in private equity -trade sales, secondary sales, initial public offerings, promoter buybacks, recapitalizations, and hybrid exits. It dives into the complex process of exit preparation, examines how firms evaluate timing and buyer selection, and analyzes the nuances of executing exits in India.

It also reflects on the psychological and strategic challenges that define this final stage of the investment lifecycle.

The Philosophy of Exiting: When Value Meets Realization

Every private equity investment begins with a blueprint for value creation and an expectation of eventual realization. Yet the path from investment to exit is rarely linear. Markets shift, strategies evolve, competitors emerge, and unforeseen events force adaptation. By the time an exit becomes possible, the company may be very different from the one the firm originally acquired.

Exiting is best understood as a philosophical exercise in timing, judgment, and alignment. The private equity firm must constantly evaluate whether the company is optimized for sale, whether additional improvements would meaningfully enhance valuation, and whether market conditions favor an exit. The firm must weigh the diminishing marginal value of holding the asset against the diminishing returns of delaying investor distributions. It must consider the maturity of its fund, the expectations of its limited partners, the appetite of strategic buyers, and the overall health of capital markets.

Timing, more than any other factor, shapes exit outcomes. A company sold during a market upswing, when multiples are expanding and buyer confidence is high, may achieve a valuation far above intrinsic value. A company sold during a downturn may struggle to attract bids even if its fundamentals are strong. Private equity firms therefore operate with a dual lens: they assess both micro-level readiness -performance, stability, scalability -and macro-level conditions -interest rates, liquidity, sector trends, and geopolitical factors.

Yet timing is not always under the firm's control. Fund life cycles impose constraints. A ten-year fund cannot hold an asset indefinitely; LPs expect liquidity. If an asset matures late in the fund's life, the firm may be compelled to pursue a sale even if markets are not ideal. This tension between fund discipline and market conditions is one of the defining strategic challenges of private equity.

Exit Readiness: Crafting the Narrative and Perfecting the Company

Exit readiness is not a moment but a multi-year process. It begins long before the first banker is engaged or the first buyer appears. It is woven into the fabric of portfolio management -through governance improvements, operational upgrades, financial discipline, and technology modernization. By the time the firm formally prepares for exit, much of the work should already be done.

However, exit preparation demands a heightened level of rigor and polish. Investors must ensure that the company presents itself with clarity, confidence, and credibility. This preparation typically involves several dimensions.

First, the company's financial reporting must be impeccable. Audited financials must reflect consistency, transparency, and accuracy. Forecasts must be credible and supported by detailed assumptions. Key performance indicators must be clearly defined and reliably tracked. Private equity firms often prep the company for "public company readiness" even if they do not plan an IPO -strengthening internal controls, documentation, disclosure practices, and audit standards.

Second, the company's strategy must be articulated with clarity. Buyers must understand the company's competitive advantages, market positioning, growth opportunities, and long-term value creation potential. Private equity firms help refine the strategic narrative -highlighting how the company has evolved, which capabilities have been built, and which opportunities remain.

Third, operational improvements must be embedded. The exit process is not the time to unveil superficial enhancements. Buyers can detect window dressing. What matters is genuine, long-term operational change -cost discipline, supply chain resilience, scalable processes, digital maturity, and leadership depth.

Fourth, leadership must be stable and aligned. Buyers want assurance that the management team is capable and committed. Private equity firms often formalize long-term incentive plans, strengthen succession pipelines, and ensure clarity around post-exit roles. Investors may introduce new leaders before the exit or ensure that existing leaders are supported to continue through the transition.

Finally, documentation must be comprehensive. Buyers will conduct rigorous due diligence. A company that is well-prepared, well-organized, and transparent accelerates the process and enhances buyer confidence. Legal, tax, environmental, commercial, and operational data must be meticulously maintained.

Exit readiness is a reflection of stewardship. It signals whether the private equity firm has truly professionalized the company or merely optimized metrics for short-term gain.

Trade Sales: Strategic Exits to Industry Buyers

Trade sales -exits to strategic buyers -represent one of the most common and often the most lucrative exit routes. Strategic buyers are companies within the same industry or adjacent industries that seek acquisitions to strengthen their competitive position. They evaluate a private equity-owned company not merely as a standalone asset but as a vehicle for synergy, expansion, and long-term strategic fit.

Strategic buyers may value the company more highly than financial investors because they see opportunity in integrating operations, cross-selling products, accessing new geographies, consolidating market share, or acquiring technologies or capabilities. These synergies often justify higher valuations and more aggressive bidding.

The strategic sale process requires careful buyer selection. Private equity firms analyze which companies would view the asset as strategically accretive, which have the financial capacity to pursue acquisitions, and which are pursuing active M&A strategies. They also assess whether potential buyers possess cultural alignment and operational fit.

Negotiations with strategic buyers are complex. They often require detailed synergy analyses, integration planning, and employee transition considerations. Strategic buyers conduct exhaustive diligence, evaluating whether the acquired company will strengthen their long-term positioning. Private equity firms must ensure that the company's systems, culture, and operations are robust enough to withstand this scrutiny.

In India, trade sales have grown significantly, with global corporations acquiring Indian businesses to access a large and growing market. Sectors such as pharmaceuticals, IT services, consumer goods, and financial services have seen notable strategic exits. Indian conglomerates have also become active acquirers, seeking to enhance scale or expand into new categories.

Trade sales, when executed well, can deliver exceptional outcomes. But they require careful timing, strong relationships, meticulous preparation, and a narrative that resonates with strategic motives.

Secondary Sales: The Rise of PE-to-PE Exits

Secondary sales -where one private equity firm sells to another -have become increasingly common as the industry matures. These transactions reflect the growing specialization within private equity.

One firm may excel at early-stage business building, while another excels at scaling mature companies. A growth equity firm may sell to a buyout firm. A buyout firm may sell to a long-hold or infrastructure-style investor. Each firm brings a different value-creation toolkit.

Secondary sales also reflect the evolution of risk appetites. A company that carries execution risk -requiring operational improvements -may be acquired by a firm with specialists in that domain. Once stabilized and scaled, the company may be attractive to a firm seeking predictable cash flows. Secondary buyers may also have access to cheaper capital, enabling them to pay higher valuations.

Executing a secondary sale requires deep understanding of the buyer universe. Private equity firms must know which investors specialize in the company's lifecycle stage, geography, and sector. They must present a clear handoff narrative: how the company has grown under their ownership and what untapped opportunities remain for the next owner.

In India, secondary sales have grown rapidly. The market has matured to the point where multiple firms at different lifecycle stages -growth equity, mid-market buyouts, large buyouts, and long-term investors -create successive ownership tiers. These transactions enhance liquidity and stabilize the ecosystem.

Secondary sales offer flexibility. They avoid public market volatility and often close faster than IPOs or strategic sales. But they demand careful positioning, as financial buyers are disciplined and valuation-sensitive.

Initial Public Offerings: Taking a Company Public

An initial public offering (IPO) is often viewed as the most prestigious exit route. It signals that the company has matured, achieved scale, stabilized governance, and built a track record worthy of public scrutiny. An IPO requires exceptional preparation. The company must meet stringent regulatory requirements, strengthen its board, maintain consistent financial performance, and articulate a compelling equity story to institutional and retail investors.

The IPO process has multiple stages -appointing bankers, preparing the red herring prospectus, conducting roadshows, engaging with analysts, and navigating regulatory approvals. Private equity firms play a central role in crafting the narrative presented to the market, highlighting performance improvements, future growth, competitive advantages, and industry tailwinds.

Yet IPOs carry risks. Public markets can be volatile. Macroeconomic shifts, geopolitical events, or interest rate changes can derail the process. Even after listing, the company must maintain quarterly performance discipline. Lock-up periods restrict the private equity firm's ability to sell shares immediately, exposing it to market fluctuations.

In India, IPOs have become more viable as capital markets deepen and investors embrace high-growth companies. Several private-equity-backed companies have successfully listed across technology, consumer, financial services, and manufacturing sectors. However, the Indian IPO market can be cyclical, with windows opening and closing rapidly. Timing is critical.

An IPO represents more than a financial transaction; it is a moment of transformation. The company becomes accountable to public shareholders, analysts, and regulators. Private equity ownership must transition to a new governance regime, often requiring additional handholding during the initial quarters as the company adapts to the public environment.

Promoter Buybacks: Returning Control to the Founders

In certain cases, founders or promoters may choose to buy back the private equity firm's stake at exit. This occurs when the business has matured to a point where the promoter wishes to regain full control, or when the private equity firm's presence has achieved its purpose -professionalizing the company, strengthening governance, enhancing performance, or scaling operations.

Promoter buybacks require alignment of interests. The promoter must have the financial resources or access to financing to repurchase the stake. The private equity firm must achieve a satisfactory return. Negotiations require sensitivity, as promoter relationships are often deeply personal.

In India, promoter buybacks are common in family-controlled companies. Founders often view private equity as a temporary partner -one that provides capital, governance, and expertise before eventually returning control to the family. These exits tend to be smoother, provided the relationship has remained strong throughout ownership.

Promoter buybacks offer privacy, speed, and continuity. But they may limit valuation compared to competitive auctions. The private equity firm must balance relationship considerations with fiduciary responsibility.

Recapitalizations: Extracting Value While Retaining Ownership

Recapitalization involves restructuring the company's balance sheet -often through new debt or strategic investors -to allow the private equity firm to extract partial liquidity while retaining ownership. This approach is common in Western markets but increasingly visible in India as credit markets deepen.

A recapitalization does not end the investment; it reshapes it. The private equity firm receives cash distributions while continuing to create value, often reducing its risk exposure while maintaining upside. Such structures require robust cash flows and lender confidence. They also require strategic clarity, ensuring that leverage does not impair future growth.

Exit Strategy Selection: Balancing Risk, Return, and Timing

Choosing an exit route involves evaluating multiple factors: the company's growth trajectory, buyer appetite, market cycles, competitive intensity, liquidity conditions, sector sentiment, and fund life considerations. The private equity firm must decide whether maximizing valuation, minimizing execution risk, or accelerating timeline is the priority.

In India, sector-specific dynamics heavily influence exit choices. Technology companies may favor IPOs due to high valuations and investor enthusiasm. Manufacturing companies may attract strategic buyers seeking scale. Consumer businesses may appeal to both strategics and financial buyers. Financial services firms must navigate regulatory constraints.

Exit selection is a strategic decision that reflects both historical performance and future potential. It requires precision, adaptability, and deep market understanding.

The Emotional and Psychological Dimensions of Exit

Exiting a company is not purely financial. It marks the end of a partnership -one built on collaboration, conflict, trust, and shared ambition. Management teams often feel a mix of pride and uncertainty. Founders may experience emotional dissonance as ownership transitions. Private equity professionals themselves may wrestle with the bittersweet nature of exit: the satisfaction of return realization mingled with the departure from a company they worked intensely to transform.

These emotional dynamics influence exit negotiations. A founder may resist certain buyers due to cultural misalignment. A management team may seek continuity. Private equity firms must navigate these human considerations with empathy while ensuring they fulfill fiduciary obligations.

In India, where business relationships often carry deep personal significance, emotional dynamics are particularly important. Successful exits balance financial discipline with cultural sensitivity.

Conclusion: Exit as the Ultimate Expression of Private Equity Discipline

Exiting is the moment when private equity's promises are tested against reality. It is the culmination of years of stewardship, effort, and risk-taking. A successful exit is not an accident. It is the result of rigorous preparation, disciplined execution, strong alignment, and deep understanding of markets and buyers.

The best private equity firms approach exits with foresight, not urgency. They begin preparing long before a sale is imminent. They build companies that buyers want to own, not companies decorated for temporary valuation boosts. They shape narratives based on substance, not superficial metrics. They orchestrate processes with precision, balancing speed with thoroughness.

In India, exits shape the credibility of both firms and the broader ecosystem. They signal the maturity of markets, the effectiveness of governance, and the quality of companies emerging from the private capital landscape. Strong exits attract global capital, deepen domestic participation, and fuel the next cycle of growth.

When exits are done well, they create lasting impact. Companies transition into new phases of growth, employees gain opportunities, industries consolidate or expand, and investors achieve returns that validate their faith in the private equity model. Exits are not the end of a story; they are the end of *one* chapter and the beginning of another -where the company, strengthened by years of disciplined ownership, moves into its next horizon with renewed purpose.

CHAPTER 12 - SECTORAL PERSPECTIVES IN PRIVATE EQUITY

Private equity is often described as a single asset class, but in reality, it is a vast constellation of industry-specific investment strategies. A private equity firm may employ consistent principles -diligence discipline, operational improvement, financial structuring -but no two sectors behave the same way. Consumer companies scale through brand building and distribution. Technology companies scale through product innovation and network effects. Healthcare companies grow through clinical excellence and regulatory navigation. Manufacturing companies depend on supply chain efficiency, capital intensity, and cost discipline. Financial services firms rely on risk management, compliance, and capital allocation. Each industry has its own economic engine, competitive structure, regulatory environment, and growth trajectory.

Sector dynamics profoundly influence private equity investment decisions. They shape valuation multiples, holding periods, exit options, governance complexity, and risk profiles. They also determine the type of expertise that private equity firms must possess to build conviction and create value. Over time, the industry has increasingly recognized that generalist investing -once the norm -is no longer sufficient in a world of rapid technological change, regulatory complexity, and specialized competition. The most successful private equity firms today combine broad investment acumen with deep sector knowledge, allowing them to see patterns others miss, anticipate disruptions before they emerge, and craft value creation plans tailored to the unique demands of each industry.

This chapter explores the sectoral dimension of private equity -how firms invest across consumer, technology, healthcare, industrials, financial services, infrastructure, and emerging sectors. It examines the nuances that define each sector, the strategic levers that drive value, and the challenges investors must navigate, especially in the complex, dynamic, and rapidly growing Indian market. Rather than treating sectors as static categories, it approaches them as dynamic ecosystems shaped by demographics, regulation, innovation, capital flows, and global trends.

Consumer and Retail: Navigating Demand, Brand, and Behavior

The consumer and retail sector has long attracted private equity interest because it sits at the heart of economic growth. As populations expand, incomes rise, and consumption patterns evolve, consumer businesses offer scalable models with long-term relevance. Yet consumer investing is far from straightforward. It requires a deep understanding of tastes, preferences, distribution channels, and brand loyalty -elements that defy simple quantitative analysis.

In consumer businesses, the underlying question is always: *Who is the customer, why do they buy, and will they continue to buy?* Private equity investors must not only analyze sales trends but interpret the psychology behind them. They must understand what differentiates a brand, what drives customer retention, and what vulnerabilities exist in shifting consumer sentiment. A company may show strong growth, but if it relies on fads, discounts, or narrow channels, its durability becomes questionable.

Distribution strategy plays a critical role, particularly in India, where retail is deeply fragmented. Traditional trade channels coexist with modern trade and e-commerce platforms, each with its own economics and influence. Investors must evaluate the company's ability to manage channel conflicts, optimize margins, expand distribution networks, and adapt to the digital transformation reshaping consumer behavior. E-commerce adds another layer of complexity -requiring capabilities in digital marketing, supply chain management, last-mile delivery, and customer experience.

Value creation in consumer businesses often focuses on brand strengthening, product innovation, channel expansion, pricing sophistication, and working capital optimization. Investors help companies modernize packaging, refine SKUs, increase throughput in manufacturing, and build omnichannel presence. They guide management through rigorous market research, competitive benchmarking, and category expansion strategies.

In India, consumer investing requires cultural sensitivity. Preferences vary dramatically across regions, income segments, and linguistic groups. What resonates in the south may not resonate in the north; what succeeds in urban metros may fail in tier-3 towns. Private equity firms with deep local insight can identify patterns that outsiders miss -spotting emerging categories, regional champions, or underpenetrated niches poised for growth.

Technology and SaaS: Investing at the Speed of Innovation

Technology investing has become one of the most attractive and complex areas in private equity. Software-as-a-Service (SaaS), digital platforms, fintech, edtech, and deep tech companies present compelling growth opportunities fuelled by innovation, scalability, and global market reach. Yet technology investing requires a fundamentally different mindset from traditional sectors. It demands fluency in product development cycles, user experience, network effects, data architecture, cloud infrastructure, and cybersecurity.

At the heart of technology investing lies the concept of scalability. Unlike manufacturing or consumer goods, software often exhibits near-zero marginal cost of replication. A strong product can serve thousands of customers with minimal incremental cost, enabling high gross margins and exponential growth. But scalability hinges on whether the company has achieved product-market fit -whether its product genuinely solves a problem and whether customers derive consistent value from it. Private equity investors evaluate churn rates, net retention, usage frequency, customer onboarding friction, and roadmap execution to determine product depth and stickiness.

Technology companies often compete globally. An Indian SaaS company may serve customers in North America, Europe, or Southeast Asia. This global orientation introduces new layers of diligence -comparing international pricing norms, understanding localization capabilities, assessing sales efficiency, and evaluating competitive intensity across geographies.

Value creation in SaaS companies frequently centers on improving monetization, optimizing customer acquisition costs, accelerating product development, expanding to new verticals, and professionalizing go-to-market motions. Investors must understand not only the economics of subscription models but also the culture of engineering organizations -how decisions are made, how technical debt is managed, and how innovation is prioritized.

The challenge with technology investing lies in the pace of change. Competitive landscapes can shift overnight. Disruptors may emerge unexpectedly. Regulatory shifts in data privacy or digital payments can reshape industry economics. Private equity firms must therefore maintain agility, continually re-evaluating their assumptions and supporting portfolio companies through rapid iteration.

In India, technology investing has expanded rapidly due to the country's engineering talent, global orientation, and cost advantage. Indian SaaS companies have become credible challengers to global incumbents, while consumer-tech companies have reshaped digital commerce, payments, and entertainment. Yet the Indian tech ecosystem also faces volatility, with periods of exuberant valuations followed by corrections. Navigating this cycle requires discipline, grounded conviction, and technological literacy.

Healthcare: Balancing Clinical Quality, Regulation, and Expansion

Healthcare is a sector like no other. It is shaped by human lives, stringent regulation, complex stakeholder networks, and profound ethical considerations. Private equity investors must strike a delicate balance between financial performance and clinical responsibility. They must understand that healthcare businesses succeed not only through efficiency but through trust, quality, and compliance.

Healthcare investing spans hospitals, diagnostics, medical devices, pharmaceuticals, healthcare IT, and wellness. Each subsector has distinct economics. Hospitals depend on capacity utilization, medical specialties, doctor retention, and geographic demand. Diagnostics require network density, turnaround time optimization, and brand credibility. Pharmaceuticals depend on R&D pipelines, manufacturing quality, regulatory approvals, and patent cycles.

Regulation plays an outsized role. Pricing caps, licensing requirements, clinical protocols, and quality standards shape the viability of healthcare investments. Investors must navigate accreditation systems, regulatory audits, and industry-specific compliance frameworks. In India, healthcare regulation varies significantly by state, adding another layer of complexity.

Value creation in healthcare frequently involves expanding networks, optimizing clinical processes, strengthening governance, enhancing quality systems, and investing in technology -such as electronic medical records, diagnostic automation, and telehealth platforms. Investors help hospitals design patient-centric models, reduce administrative inefficiencies, and enhance revenue cycle management. In diagnostics, they support footprint expansion, brand strengthening, and logistics optimization.

Healthcare investing also requires sensitivity to human capital. Doctors, nurses, technicians, and clinical administrators form the backbone of the industry. Their morale, training, and alignment determine quality of care. Investors must ensure that operational changes enhance rather than undermine clinical excellence.

The Indian healthcare market presents both immense opportunity and structural challenges. Rising incomes, aging populations, and chronic disease prevalence fuel demand. Yet quality varies widely, infrastructure is uneven, and affordability remains a concern. Private equity firms that invest responsibly -balancing growth with quality -can create enduring impact.

Industrials and Manufacturing: Efficiency, Scale, and Capital Intensity

Industrial and manufacturing companies operate in a world of precision, throughput, procurement, and cost discipline. These businesses often have thin margins, long capital cycles, and complex supply chains. Yet they offer stability, resilience, and significant potential for operational value creation.

Private equity investors examine plant utilization, raw material procurement, maintenance practices, inventory cycles, labor productivity, and energy consumption. They evaluate supply chain robustness, vendor relationships, quality systems, and export potential. They assess whether the company operates with modern manufacturing principles -lean, Six Sigma, total productive maintenance -or relies on outdated processes.

Value creation in industrials often revolves around cost optimization, capacity expansion, automation, digitization, and working capital discipline. Operating partners play a critical role -installing dashboards, redesigning production flows, implementing predictive maintenance, and renegotiating vendor contracts.

Manufacturing also involves navigating external risks -commodity volatility, global trade dynamics, regulatory compliance, and environmental standards. Investors must understand whether the company is exposed to cyclicality, whether it has pricing power, and whether it possesses technical differentiation.

In India, manufacturing presents unique complexities. Labor intensity is high but productivity may be inconsistent. Infrastructure gaps can affect logistics. Supply chains may be partially informal. Yet India's manufacturing potential is expanding due to rising global interest in China-plus-one strategies, government incentives, and improving infrastructure. Private equity firms that can professionalize operations and position companies for global competitiveness stand to create outsized value.

Financial Services and Fintech: Regulation, Risk, and Innovation

Financial services represent one of the most powerful sectors for private equity, combining recurring revenue, high scalability, and deep impact. The sector spans banks, NBFCs, insurance companies, asset managers, brokers, fintech platforms, and payment companies. But it is also a sector where mistakes can be catastrophic, and regulatory missteps can destroy value quickly.

Investors must understand credit risk, underwriting models, collections infrastructure, asset-liability management, compliance frameworks, and capital adequacy norms. They must analyze loan books at granular levels -by geography, segment, borrower profile, and collateral quality. They study delinquency trends, provisioning practices, and risk management systems.

Fintech adds another layer of intricacy -combining innovation with regulatory ambiguity. Payments, lending, neobanking, wealthtech, insuretech, and embedded finance create new opportunities but also new risks. Technology-driven models require deep evaluation of unit economics, fraud risk, data architecture, and customer acquisition costs.

Value creation in financial services involves strengthening risk management, improving underwriting algorithms, enhancing collections, optimizing capital structures, expanding distribution, and integrating digital tools. Investors help companies adopt analytics, improve compliance, refine pricing models, and develop partnerships.

Regulation is the defining force. In India, RBI, IRDAI, SEBI, and other agencies shape the entire ecosystem. Regulatory tightening or policy shifts can dramatically alter business models. Private equity firms must anticipate regulatory trends and invest in companies capable of navigating them responsibly.

Infrastructure and Energy: Long Horizons and Stable Cash Flows

Infrastructure and energy investments occupy a distinct space in private equity -offering long-term stability, predictable cash flows, and inflation-linked returns. They include renewable energy, logistics infrastructure, utilities, telecommunications towers, and transportation assets.

These assets require significant initial capital but generate consistent cash flows once operational. Investors evaluate contract structures, regulatory frameworks, tariff mechanisms, counterparty risks, and asset longevity. Renewable energy, especially solar and wind, has become attractive in India due to declining costs, government incentives, and climate imperatives.

Value creation involves optimizing project execution, reducing cost of capital, enhancing operational efficiency, and consolidating fragmented asset portfolios. Exit strategies often involve yield-focused investors, sovereign funds, or infrastructure platforms.

Emerging Sectors: The Frontier of Opportunity

New sectors continuously emerge at the intersection of technology, demographics, and global trends. These include climate-tech, EV ecosystems, agritech, supply chain digitization, semiconductors, AI-driven enterprises, and space-tech. Investing in such frontier sectors requires a blend of vision, technical literacy, and risk appetite.

Private equity firms must evaluate technological feasibility, regulatory frameworks, capital requirements, and ecosystem readiness. These sectors may lack historical data, requiring investors to build conviction through first-principles thinking rather than traditional benchmarking.

India is becoming a fertile ground for emerging sectors, driven by youthful demographics, entrepreneurial energy, and government initiatives. Private equity firms open to early specialization can shape the next generation of category leaders.

Conclusion: Sector Specialization as a Strategic Imperative

Sectoral perspectives are no longer optional in private equity -they are central to success. Each sector operates with its own rules, rhythms, and risk patterns. Each requires a different lens of analysis, a different style of value creation, and a different approach to governance. Sector expertise strengthens conviction, enhances sourcing advantages, improves diligence accuracy, deepens value creation, and sharpens exit strategies.

In India, sector specialization is especially critical due to the country's diversity, regulatory variability, and rapid evolution. Firms that understand sectoral nuances can identify untapped opportunities long before they become widely visible. They can navigate informal structures, anticipate consumer shifts, and build companies that are globally competitive.

Ultimately, private equity is not about applying generic frameworks to generic companies. It is about understanding the unique engines that drive each industry and shaping them with the discipline and imagination that define the asset class. Sectoral depth turns private equity from a financial exercise into a strategic craft, enabling investors to create enduring value across the vast tapestry of the modern economy.

CHAPTER 13 - RISK MANAGEMENT IN PRIVATE EQUITY

Private equity is often celebrated for its value creation prowess, its active ownership model, and its ability to generate outsized returns. Yet beneath the surface of every successful investment lies a complex architecture of risk management -an intricate system of discipline, foresight, judgment, and structured decision-making. Risk in private equity is not an occasional hazard; it is the constant background condition of the asset class. Every decision, from the earliest stages of sourcing to the final exit, carries uncertainty. Markets shift, customers evolve, competitors respond, regulations tighten, technologies disrupt, and macroeconomic environments fluctuate. The art of private equity lies not in avoiding risk -such avoidance would lead to inactivity and missed opportunities -but in understanding risk deeply enough to price it, mitigate it, and ultimately transform it into controlled opportunity.

Unlike public markets, where risk is often measured through volatility, beta, or price fluctuations, private equity risk is far more qualitative and multidimensional. It resides in business models, leadership teams, operational structures, debt loads, supply chains, compliance frameworks, technology stacks, and competitive positions. It resides in human behavior, incentives, and organizational culture. It resides in macroeconomic conditions, geopolitical shifts, capital markets, and regulatory regimes. Private equity firms therefore adopt a holistic view of risk, integrating analytical rigor with contextual understanding and hands-on operational insight.

This chapter explores the philosophy and practice of risk management in private equity. It examines how firms identify, evaluate, mitigate, and monitor risk across the investment process -from sourcing and diligence to ownership and exit. It contextualizes these dynamics within the Indian market, where complexities in regulation, governance, and business practices create unique risk profiles. Ultimately, the chapter argues that risk management is not merely a protective function but a core enabler of high-quality investing.

The Philosophy of Risk: Embracing Uncertainty with Discipline

Risk is often misunderstood as something to be minimized or avoided. Yet private equity, by design, seeks opportunity in environments where uncertainty exists. If outcomes were predictable, returns would be low and competition intense. The essence of private equity lies in identifying companies with imperfect structures, incomplete capabilities, or underappreciated potential -and transforming them into more valuable enterprises. This transformation inherently involves taking risk.

The true objective of risk management in private equity is therefore not risk elimination but risk understanding. What matters is clarity: clarity about the magnitude of risk, clarity about its sources, and clarity about how it interacts with value creation plans. Investors must distinguish between risks that can be mitigated through action, risks that can be priced into the acquisition, and risks that are unacceptable given the firm's mandate.

This philosophy gives rise to three guiding principles.

First, *risk must be examined holistically*, not in isolated categories. A company with strong financial performance but weak governance may be riskier than a company with moderate financials and excellent governance.

Second, *risk evolves over time*, and must be continually reassessed. What is low risk at acquisition may become high risk under changing market conditions.

Third, *risk and return are inherently linked*; higher-return strategies typically involve greater complexity, transformation, or cyclicality.

The goal is not to fear risk but to bring it into the light -to interrogate it, quantify it where possible, and embed it within a coherent investment thesis.

Risk at the Sourcing Stage: Identifying the Right Kind of Opportunities

Risk management begins long before diligence starts. The types of deals a private equity firm chooses to pursue reflect its philosophy, capabilities, and organizational appetite. Sector focus, deal size, geographic footprint, and investment style all shape the baseline risk profile.

Firms with strong operating capabilities may pursue underperforming assets requiring turnaround. Firms with deep sector expertise may pursue technically complex businesses that others avoid. Conversely, firms with limited operational bandwidth may prefer high-quality growth businesses with fewer moving parts. Some firms avoid cyclical sectors entirely; others specialize in them.

The sourcing stage also requires awareness of selection risk -the risk of pursuing opportunities that do not truly fit the firm's strategy. In India, where deal flow is abundant and diverse, this discipline is vital. Investors must avoid being seduced by brand names, temporary growth spurts, or market excitement. They must filter opportunities through both strategic alignment and long-term feasibility.

By exercising discipline at the sourcing stage, firms avoid downstream risks that emerge from misaligned mandates, inadequate sector knowledge, or overconfidence.

Risk During Due Diligence: Discovering and Diagnosing the Truth

Due diligence is the most structured and rigorous phase of risk assessment. It is when private equity firms examine the company's financials, commercial environment, operations, technology, legal compliance, tax obligations, and ESG practices. Each dimension holds risk, and each must be evaluated not in isolation but in relation to the investment thesis.

Financial diligence surfaces risks related to revenue concentration, margin sustainability, working capital volatility, accounting practices, and cash conversion. A business with strong EBITDA but inconsistent cash flow may be exposed to hidden operational inefficiencies. A company with high margins may face competitive pressure that erodes pricing power. Diligence reveals the stability -or fragility -of the economic engine.

Commercial diligence evaluates whether the company's market positioning is durable. Risks emerge from changing customer behavior, new competitors, substitute technologies, regulatory shifts, or evolving industry structures. For example, a consumer brand may appear strong but rely heavily on one distribution channel vulnerable to disruption. A SaaS company may grow rapidly but suffer from unsustainably high customer acquisition costs.

Operational diligence surfaces risks in manufacturing efficiency, supply chain reliability, quality control, labor productivity, and technological readiness. Investors must understand whether operations can scale profitably and whether operational weaknesses pose long-term threats. A seemingly small operational flaw can significantly impact valuation if it affects pricing, customer satisfaction, or compliance.

Legal and tax diligence uncovers risks that may not be visible in financial statements -land ownership disputes, licensing issues, compliance lapses, contingent liabilities, or tax exposures. In India, such risks require heightened scrutiny due to complex regulatory frameworks and historical informality.

Technology diligence reveals risks related to scalability, data security, product stability, and technical debt. In a digital world, weak technology foundations can severely limit long-term growth.

ESG diligence identifies environmental, labor, safety, and governance risks. These may not impact short-term numbers but can significantly affect long-term sustainability and exit attractiveness.

Diligence seeks to differentiate between manageable risk -where mitigation plans can be implemented -and unacceptable risk, where the investment must be abandoned. It is the investigative laboratory in which thesis, reality, and risk converge.

Risk at the Deal Structuring Stage: Pricing and Protection

Even after diligence, risk remains. Deal structuring allows private equity firms to embed risk-sharing mechanisms and protective frameworks into transaction documents. Pricing is the first line of defense: riskier companies must be acquired at valuations that reflect uncertainty. An aggressively priced deal leaves little margin for error.

Beyond pricing, private equity firms shape deal terms to protect themselves. Shareholder agreements include clauses related to governance, reporting, veto rights, liquidation preferences, antidilution, indemnities, and exit rights. The degree of control a firm obtains reflects its assessment of risk. In minority deals, particularly common in India, investors rely heavily on contractual protections to safeguard their interests.

For leveraged buyouts, capital structure is a central dimension of risk. Excessive leverage amplifies risk dramatically. Firms must balance the benefits of debt -enhanced returns, tax efficiency -with the risks of over-commitment. Sensitivity analyses, stress testing, and cash flow modelling guide decisions on leverage levels.

In India, structuring risk is influenced by regulatory restrictions on foreign investment, sectoral caps, tax considerations, and promoter dynamics. The ability to structure effectively becomes a competitive advantage.

Risk During Ownership: Monitoring, Managing, and Mitigating

Once the deal closes, risk does not diminish -it changes form. The ownership phase introduces new risks: execution risk, cultural risk, leadership risk, operational drift, compliance slippage, and market evolution. Private equity firms must actively manage these risks through governance, monitoring, and engagement.

Governance is the cornerstone of risk oversight. Regular board meetings, detailed reporting, KPI dashboards, and committee structures ensure transparency. Investors gain visibility into trends before they become crises. Early detection is critical; a stagnating sales funnel, deteriorating margin trend, or rising attrition rate may signal deeper issues.

Leadership risk is particularly important. The CEO's capability, alignment, and decision-making influence the entire company. Private equity firms may need to replace or augment leadership teams during ownership. Such transitions are delicate but often necessary to mitigate long-term risk.

Operational risk emerges as companies scale. Processes that worked for a smaller company may fail under complexity. Technology systems may lag growth. Supply chains may become strained. Private equity firms deploy operating partners to strengthen processes, reduce waste, professionalize teams, and modernize systems.

Cultural risk is subtler but equally important. Rapid change can create fear, resistance, or disengagement. A toxic or misaligned culture jeopardizes performance. Investors must balance urgency with empathy, shaping a culture of accountability without creating organizational fatigue.

Regulatory and compliance risk requires constant vigilance. Especially in India, where regulations evolve frequently, companies must maintain agility and strong internal controls. Compliance failures can result in fines, litigation, debarment, or reputational damage that affects exit value.

Cybersecurity has become a significant source of risk. Data breaches, ransomware attacks, and system failures pose existential threats. Technology diligence must be followed by ongoing cyber risk monitoring.

Macroeconomic risk extends beyond the company. Interest rate changes affect leverage costs. Inflation influences input prices. Currency volatility affects exporters. Geopolitical shifts affect supply chains. Private equity firms incorporate macro scenarios into strategic planning and financial forecasting.

Throughout ownership, risk management is not reactive -it is anticipatory. The best firms identify leading indicators, not just lagging ones. They intervene early, communicate clearly, and adapt quickly.

Risk at Exit: Timing, Market Sentiment, and Execution Complexity

Exit is a moment of crystallization. Years of work and accumulated risk culminate in a single decision: when and how to sell. Timing risk is paramount. Market windows can open and close rapidly. Sector sentiment can shift abruptly. Capital market conditions may influence valuations dramatically.

Private equity firms must evaluate whether the company has reached a state of stability, scalability, and attractiveness that will command strong buyer interest. They must judge whether additional improvements will yield meaningful valuation uplift or merely introduce delay.

Different exit routes carry different risk profiles. Trade sales depend on strategic alignment and synergy potential. Secondary sales depend on sponsor appetite and sector outlook. IPOs depend on public market sentiment, analyst coverage, regulatory frameworks, and quarterly performance visibility. Promoter buybacks depend on financing capacity and negotiation dynamics.

Execution risk is significant. Exits require meticulous preparation -audits, documentation, management narratives, data rooms, banker engagement, investor education, and due diligence readiness. A poorly prepared company may attract lower bids or lose credibility with buyers.

In India, exit risk is influenced by market depth, regulatory clarity, buyer sophistication, and currency stability. IPO markets, in particular, oscillate between exuberance and hesitation. Private equity firms must navigate these cycles with sensitivity and foresight.

Cross-Cutting Risks: Governance, Culture, Technology, and ESG

Certain risks cut across sectors and stages. Governance risk is one of the most significant. Weak governance leads to poor decisions, compliance failures, and strategic drift. Private equity firms must establish strong audit controls, reporting systems, and board structures.

Culture risk arises when organizations resist change or fail to attract talent. Cultural transformation requires careful leadership, communication, and incentive alignment.

Technology risk grows each year. Companies that ignore digital transformation face obsolescence. Companies with poor cybersecurity face existential threats. Technology must be embedded in value creation plans, not treated as a secondary consideration.

ESG risk has become increasingly critical. Investors, regulators, customers, and buyers demand responsible practices. Poor ESG performance limits exit options, particularly with global buyers. Private equity firms must integrate ESG from diligence through ownership.

The Indian Context: Risk in a High-Growth, High-Complexity Market

India presents unique risk dynamics. The market offers immense growth potential but is characterized by regulatory complexity, informal practices, regional diversity, and rapid change. Promoter dynamics add another layer -founders may maintain significant influence even after private equity investment. Investors must manage alignment carefully.

Tax and legal frameworks are detailed and frequently updated, requiring ongoing compliance. Competition is intense, often with local players adopting aggressive tactics. Infrastructure gaps affect logistics and supply chains. Yet these complexities create opportunities for investors who can navigate them with sophistication.

Risk in India is not a deterrent; it is a differentiator. Firms that master Indian risk dynamics gain an advantage over global competitors who underestimate the importance of local nuance.

Conclusion: Risk as the Lens Through Which Great Private Equity Firms See the World

Risk management is not merely a defensive activity; it is the central discipline that underpins private equity excellence. Great private equity firms are defined by their ability to see risks clearly, price them correctly, mitigate them intelligently, and convert them into structured opportunities for value creation. They remain intellectually honest even when excited about a deal. They challenge assumptions, embrace scepticism, and encourage transparency. They recognize that risk evolves and that vigilance must be continuous.

In the end, private equity success is not about avoiding risk -it is about understanding it more deeply than others. It is about navigating uncertainty with clarity, courage, and discipline. It is about transforming imperfect companies into stronger, more resilient enterprises. And it is about building the conviction necessary to make bold decisions while safeguarding the interests of investors, employees, customers, and stakeholders.

Risk is the compass of private equity. When understood and managed wisely, it becomes not a constraint, but a source of strength -the foundation upon which sustainable returns, responsible stewardship, and long-term value creation are built.

CHAPTER 14 - ESG AND RESPONSIBLE INVESTING IN PRIVATE EQUITY

Private equity has historically been associated with financial engineering, operational improvement, strategic transformation, and value creation. But in recent years, a profound evolution has taken place -one that has broadened the definition of value itself. Investors, governments, regulators, customers, and society at large now expect private equity firms to consider not only financial returns but also the environmental, social, and governance impact of the companies they own. ESG, once a peripheral concept, has moved to the center of private equity strategy. It shapes how funds are raised, how companies are selected, how value is created, and how exits are achieved. It influences reputation, risk, regulation, and long-term performance.

The rise of ESG is not a passing trend. It reflects a structural shift in how businesses operate, how capital is allocated, and how stakeholders judge corporate success. Climate change, social inequality, digital privacy, governance failures, and regulatory tightening have made ESG not simply an ethical preference but a business imperative. In this environment, private equity's active ownership model -its ability to influence strategy, governance, operations, and culture -positions it uniquely to drive responsible transformation.

This chapter explores the meaning, significance, and practice of ESG in private equity. It examines how ESG influences fundraising, diligence, value creation, and exit. It delves into the complexities of integrating ESG into investment processes, the challenges of measurement and reporting, and the nuances of ESG in the Indian market. More importantly, it argues that responsible investing is not merely about doing good; it is about building resilient companies that can thrive in a world defined by disruption, transparency, and sustainability.

The Emergence of ESG as a Core Investment Principle

ESG's rise in private equity reflects broader societal and economic forces. Over the past two decades, climate science has highlighted alarming risks, consumers have demanded ethical behavior, employees have sought purpose-driven companies, and regulators have tightened standards across industries. Institutional investors -pension funds, sovereign wealth funds, endowments -have responded by integrating ESG into their mandates. They allocate capital to managers who demonstrate strong ESG frameworks and withhold capital from those who ignore sustainability risks.

As a result, ESG has become a screening criterion in fundraising. Limited partners expect private equity firms to articulate ESG policies, provide evidence of implementation, and offer transparency on impact. What was once a marketing soundbite is now evaluated with rigor. Investment committees within LP institutions increasingly include ESG specialists who examine fund practices in detail.

This shift in expectations has created a powerful incentive: private equity firms that excel in ESG attract more capital, particularly from global institutions. Conversely, firms that fail to adapt risk exclusion from funding pools. ESG is now baked into the very economics of the private capital ecosystem.

The philosophical shift is equally important. ESG challenges the traditional assumption that financial value and societal value must be traded off. Instead, it posits that companies with sustainable practices -strong governance, ethical operations, environmental responsibility -are more resilient, less risky, and more valuable in the long run. This reframing aligns ESG with private equity's fundamental mission: building stronger, more competitive companies.

Understanding the Three Pillars: Environment, Social, and Governance

ESG consists of three interconnected dimensions -environmental, social, and governance. Yet these pillars are not abstract ideas; they are embodied in the operations, culture, and trajectory of every company.

The environmental dimension concerns a company's impact on the natural world. This includes energy usage, emissions, waste management, resource efficiency, pollution controls, water consumption, and climate resilience. Companies with high environmental risk -heavy industries, chemicals, logistics -face regulatory pressure, reputational risk, and rising compliance costs. Companies with strong environmental stewardship often enjoy operational efficiencies, brand value, and favorable stakeholder perception.

The social dimension addresses how a company treats its employees, customers, suppliers, and communities. Labor practices, health and safety, diversity and inclusion, human rights, data privacy, customer fairness, and community engagement all fall under this umbrella. Social risk can be subtle but devastating -a toxic workplace culture, unsafe factories, discriminatory practices, or privacy violations can destroy value quickly.

Governance is the backbone of ESG. It concerns leadership integrity, board structure, transparency, accountability, internal controls, ethical conduct, and shareholder rights. Governance failures lie behind some of the largest corporate collapses in history. A company with strong governance is less likely to face fraud, compliance breaches, operational disasters, or cultural decay.

In private equity, the governance pillar is particularly influential because it is the one area where investors can directly intervene. Unlike public shareholders, private equity owners control board appointments, influence leadership decisions, enforce transparency, and drive structural improvements.

ESG in Fundraising: A New Standard for Accountability

Fundraising is increasingly shaped by ESG considerations. Limited partners expect private equity firms to demonstrate responsible stewardship. During fundraising, LPs evaluate the firm's ESG frameworks -policies, procedures, reporting, and track record. They want to know whether ESG is embedded into the DNA of the firm or treated as a superficial compliance requirement.

Private equity firms now develop ESG policies that articulate commitments to responsible investing. These policies outline how the firm integrates ESG into sourcing, diligence, value creation, and monitoring. They define exclusion lists -sectors or practices that the firm will not invest in due to environmental harm, ethical concerns, or governance risk. They establish responsibilities within the firm -appointing ESG officers, forming ESG committees, and training investment professionals.

Fundraising due diligence often involves detailed questionnaires on ESG capabilities. LPs ask how the firm identifies ESG risks, whether it collects data from portfolio companies, how it handles incidents, how it measures impact, and how it reports progress. They seek evidence of ESG in action -case studies demonstrating how the firm improved safety practices, reduced emissions, strengthened governance, or addressed social issues.

Private equity firms that cannot respond convincingly risk losing commitments. In some cases, global LPs require ESG alignment as a condition of allocation.

ESG has therefore shifted from a differentiating factor to a baseline requirement. It is a license to operate in modern private markets.

ESG in Due Diligence: Discovering Risks and Opportunities

ESG diligence has become a standard component of pre-investment analysis. Just as financial, commercial, and operational diligence uncover hidden risks, ESG diligence examines the company's sustainability profile. It reveals liabilities that could undermine value creation or prevent future exit.

Environmental diligence may identify deficiencies in pollution controls, outdated equipment, hazardous waste management, illegal water usage, or climate vulnerability. Correcting these issues may require significant investment, altering valuation assumptions.

Social diligence uncovers risks related to employee safety, labor law compliance, turnover patterns, discrimination, harassment, or human rights violations in supply chains. Such risks can lead to legal penalties or reputational damage.

Governance diligence evaluates board structure, transparency, internal controls, compliance mechanisms, related-party transactions, historical controversies, and ethical standards. In India, governance issues are particularly prevalent due to promoter dominance, informal practices, and limited board independence.

Importantly, ESG diligence also uncovers *opportunities*. Companies with strong ESG profiles may benefit from customer trust, better talent retention, operational efficiency, lower regulatory risk, and differentiated brand identity. Some ESG strengths -such as renewable energy usage, DEI leadership, or sustainable sourcing -can command valuation premiums.

Private equity firms use ESG diligence to shape investment decisions, negotiate valuation adjustments, establish early-warning systems, and design value creation plans that incorporate sustainability improvements.

ESG Integration During Ownership: Creating Sustainable Value

The ownership phase is where ESG becomes truly transformative. Private equity firms can influence company strategy, redesign processes, and shift culture. ESG integration moves beyond risk mitigation into value creation.

Environmental improvements may involve energy efficiency projects, sustainable sourcing, emissions reduction, waste minimization, green certifications, or circular economy initiatives. These changes often reduce cost, enhance efficiency, and improve brand reputation.

Social initiatives may include workforce safety enhancements, structured HR processes, diversity programs, employee training, community engagement, and improved customer experience. Companies with strong employee engagement outperform those with toxic cultures. Companies with inclusive practices attract superior talent.

Governance transformation is often the most impactful. Private equity firms strengthen boards with independent directors, formalize delegation frameworks, establish audit committees, mandate clean reporting, and embed whistleblower systems. They eliminate related-party transactions, formalize documentation, and introduce transparency. Governance upgrades protect the company from fraud, corruption, or mismanagement.

In India, the governance uplift provided by private equity has been transformative. Many founder-run businesses lack formal processes. Private equity firms help them professionalize, institutionalize, and prepare for long-term growth or public listing.

ESG becomes part of the company's identity -not a compliance requirement but a competitive advantage.

Measurement and Reporting: The Challenge of Quantifying ESG

One of the most difficult aspects of ESG is measurement. Unlike financial metrics, which are standardized, ESG metrics vary widely across industries, geographies, and frameworks. Measuring emissions, diversity, employee satisfaction, governance quality, or supply-chain ethics requires subjective judgment.

Private equity firms typically adopt internationally recognized frameworks -SASB, TCFD, GRI, UNPRI, IFC Performance Standards -to standardize reporting. They design ESG scorecards, collect data from portfolio companies, conduct audits, and review progress regularly.

Measurement serves three purposes.

First, it provides transparency to LPs, demonstrating that the firm takes ESG seriously.

Second, it gives companies a baseline for improvement.

Third, it strengthens exit readiness -buyers increasingly demand ESG evidence.

The challenge lies in balancing thoroughness with practicality. Excessive reporting can overwhelm management teams. Poorly defined metrics can mislead investors. The goal is to measure what truly matters, not to chase ESG checklists.

ESG and Exit Value: Why Sustainability Enhances Liquidity

ESG influences exit outcomes both directly and indirectly. Buyers -whether strategic, financial, or public market investors -prefer companies with strong ESG profiles. ESG reduces risk, enhances brand value, improves operational efficiency, and signals responsible governance. Companies with strong ESG practices often command higher valuations and attract more bidder interest.

Strategic buyers increasingly evaluate ESG alignment with their sustainability commitments. Many multinational companies will not acquire businesses that fail to meet environmental or labor standards. Strong ESG performance therefore broadens the buyer universe.

Secondary buyers -other private equity firms -demand transparency on ESG risks and prefer companies with improved processes and compliance.

IPO markets are especially sensitive to ESG. Public shareholders scrutinize governance quality, board independence, climate commitments, and social responsibility. Regulators require detailed disclosures. Companies weak in ESG may face valuation discounts or investor resistance.

Thus, ESG is no longer a cost; it is an asset that strengthens exit positioning.

ESG in India: Complexity, Urgency, and Opportunity

India presents a distinctive ESG landscape. The country faces significant environmental challenges -pollution, water scarcity, waste management, and climate vulnerability. Social issues such as workforce safety, informal labor, inequality, and diversity require attention. Governance has historically been inconsistent in promoter-driven companies. These challenges create risks but also massive opportunities.

Private equity plays a vital role in elevating ESG standards in India. Investors help companies build formal processes, strengthen compliance, professionalize management, and adopt sustainability initiatives. They support companies in achieving global certifications, improving safety, reducing emissions, and enhancing governance.

India's regulatory environment is evolving rapidly, with increasing emphasis on sustainability disclosures, ESG ratings, and corporate governance reforms. Companies with strong ESG practices are better positioned for long-term success.

The Indian market also offers ESG-driven growth sectors -renewable energy, electric mobility, healthcare, education, water management, waste recycling, sustainable agriculture, climate-tech, and fintech for financial inclusion. Private equity firms that embrace ESG can participate in this transformation meaningfully.

Conclusion: ESG as the Future of Private Equity

ESG is not an adjunct to private equity; it is becoming one of its defining pillars. It shapes how capital is raised, how deals are evaluated, how companies are managed, how value is created, and how exits are executed. It strengthens governance, enhances resilience, reduces risk, and improves long-term performance.

But more importantly, ESG aligns private equity with global imperatives. As the world confronts environmental challenges, social inequalities, and governance failures, private equity's ability to influence companies becomes a powerful force for responsibility and sustainability.

The firms that integrate ESG deeply -not as a box-ticking exercise but as a core investment philosophy -will attract more capital, create more resilient companies, and deliver superior long-term returns. ESG is not the opposite of profit; it is the pathway to sustainable profit in a world where responsibility is inseparable from success.

Private equity, when practiced responsibly, becomes not only a generator of financial value but a steward of societal progress. ESG is the lens that allows the industry to fulfill this higher purpose.

CHAPTER 15 - CROSS-BORDER PRIVATE EQUITY INVESTING

Private equity has long outgrown its origins as a domestic investment discipline. Today it is a global system -one in which capital flows seamlessly across continents, firms operate internationally, and value creation transcends geographic boundaries. Globalization has reshaped private equity by giving firms access to a vastly expanded universe of opportunities, talent, and capital. It has enabled the growth of multinational portfolios, cross-border mergers and acquisitions, and international expansion strategies. Yet at the same time, cross-border investing introduces profound complexity -legal, regulatory, cultural, operational, financial, and geopolitical.

Cross-border private equity investing is not merely an extension of domestic investing. It requires a fundamentally different lens -one that integrates global macroeconomics with local market nuance, international governance standards with national regulatory idiosyncrasies, and cross-cultural collaboration with on-the-ground operational discipline. Firms that succeed in cross-border investing demonstrate not only analytical sophistication but cultural fluency, geopolitical awareness, and flexibility in navigating unfamiliar systems.

This chapter explores the landscape of cross-border private equity investing. It examines the strategic motivations for global investment, the hurdles and opportunities inherent in international dealmaking, the complexities of managing cross-border portfolios, and the specific dynamics shaping India's role in the global private equity ecosystem. It also highlights the risks that arise when investing across borders and the skills required to execute such strategies responsibly and effectively.

The Rise of Global Private Equity: Capital Without Borders

Private equity began as a largely domestic, relationship-driven industry. But as the asset class matured, capital began to seek global diversification. Institutional investors -pension funds, sovereign wealth funds, and endowments -faced mounting obligations, prompting them to explore growth in emerging markets and diversify their exposures beyond home economies. Private equity firms responded by expanding internationally, establishing offices in London, Hong Kong, Mumbai, Singapore, Dubai, São Paulo, and beyond.

This shift was driven by two fundamental forces.

First, developed markets had begun to exhibit lower growth rates, compressing return expectations. Investors seeking higher returns looked toward emerging markets with younger populations, rising consumption, and rapid industrialization. Second, globalization integrated supply chains, technologies, and financial markets, enabling firms to create value from international synergies, cross-border expansion, and multinational optimization.

The result has been a truly global private equity ecosystem. Global firms invest across continents. Mid-market firms seek exposure to high-growth markets outside their home base. Sovereign funds and pension funds establish direct investment teams in foreign countries. Cross-border deals become increasingly common, with companies themselves becoming global in structure, talent, and ambition.

Private equity is no longer a collection of national markets -it is a global architecture of capital, expertise, and opportunity.

Motivations for Cross-Border Investing: Growth, Diversification, and Strategic Advantage

Cross-border private equity investing is not a random exploration. It is driven by clear strategic motivations. Firms seek international exposure because it offers access to growth, diversification of risk, and competitive advantage.

One of the most compelling reasons is growth. Emerging markets like India, China, Southeast Asia, Africa, and Latin America offer demographic tailwinds, consumption growth, infrastructure investment, urbanization, and digital penetration. These markets present opportunities that are often absent in slow-growth developed economies. Private equity firms pursue sectors such as healthcare, financial services, consumer goods, logistics, renewable energy, and technology, where growth trajectories are steep.

Diversification is another critical driver. Investing across borders reduces reliance on a single economic cycle. When one region experiences slowdown, others may be expanding. This diversification is valuable for institutional investors seeking stable, risk-adjusted returns across decades.

Cross-border investing also enhances strategic advantage. Firms that operate internationally gain exposure to best practices from multiple markets. They can cross-pollinate ideas -applying operational models from the US to companies in India, leveraging technological innovation from Europe in Asian markets, or enabling portfolio companies to expand globally. Cross-border collaboration allows for synergy creation, knowledge transfer, and brand building.

Finally, cross-border investing may arise from global acquisition strategies. A multinational corporation may acquire an Indian company to enter the Indian market. A private equity firm with global sector expertise may seek opportunities in new geographies to expand its sector footprint.

In each case, the motivations are strategic, not opportunistic. Private equity firms invest globally because the world offers a richer, more diverse opportunity set than any single country.

The Challenges of Cross-Border Investing: Understanding the Complexity

While the benefits of cross-border investing are considerable, the challenges are equally significant. Cross-border private equity deals require navigating unfamiliar and often unpredictable environments. The complexity arises from differences in culture, regulation, taxation, corporate governance, accounting standards, political stability, currency fluctuations, and economic structures.

Cultural complexity is one of the most underestimated yet impactful dimensions. Business norms vary widely across regions. Negotiation styles differ. Hierarchies take different forms. Communication patterns vary. For example, decisions in India may be influenced by family dynamics, informal relationships, or regional cultural norms. In the US or Europe, decisions may be more procedural and decentralized. Misreading cultural cues can lead to misunderstandings, mistrust, or misalignment with founders and management teams.

Regulatory and legal complexity introduces another layer of risk. Cross-border deals must comply with both home-country and host-country regulations. Foreign investment restrictions, sectoral caps, exchange control laws, competition rules, and tax treaties can shape deal structures significantly. For example, India's foreign direct investment (FDI) rules, Reserve Bank of India guidelines, and sector-specific regulations require careful navigation. A single regulatory misstep can derail a deal or expose the firm to long-term liability.

Currency risk can drastically alter outcomes. Exchange rate fluctuations influence returns when investments are valued or realized in local currency but repatriated in US dollars or euros. Private equity firms must incorporate currency hedging, inflation understanding, and macroeconomic modelling into their investment approach.

Operational complexity arises from distance. Managing portfolio companies across borders involves logistical challenges, time zone differences, and limited on-the-ground visibility. It requires strong local teams, effective communication systems, and governance structures suited to remote oversight.

Finally, geopolitical risk adds unpredictability. Trade tensions, sanctions, political instability, and global crises can disrupt operations or alter regulatory landscapes overnight. Private equity firms must factor geopolitical awareness into their strategy.

Cross-border investing is therefore not simply about geographic expansion -it is about managing a multi-dimensional matrix of risks and opportunities.

Local Expertise: The Foundation of Successful International Investing

The most successful private equity firms recognize that cross-border investing cannot be done effectively from a distance. Local expertise is essential. This expertise manifests not only in local offices and investment teams but also in the depth of networks, knowledge of local business culture, regulatory familiarity, and operational fluency.

Local teams help source high-quality deals -many of which are never formally marketed. They understand local market dynamics, know which founders are credible, and can assess management quality through nuanced cultural cues that outsiders might miss. They detect early signs of risk and build trust more effectively.

Moreover, local presence is essential during due diligence. Investors must verify information through site visits, customer interviews, supplier conversations, competitor insights, and local intelligence -activities that are difficult to execute without on-the-ground knowledge. In emerging markets like India, where documentation may be incomplete and informal practices common, local teams play a critical role in diligence.

Local expertise is equally important during ownership. Portfolio management requires frequent engagement with management teams, monitoring operations, guiding strategy, enhancing governance, and resolving crises. Distance weakens the investor's ability to intervene quickly or appropriately. Strong local leadership ensures that governance is enforced, value creation plans are executed, and early warning signals are captured.

Private equity firms that invest cross-border without local depth risk misjudging cultural dynamics, underestimating market complexity, or failing to execute effectively. The firms that succeed combine global perspective with local nuance.

Cross-Border Deal Structuring: Regulatory, Tax, and Legal Considerations

Structuring cross-border deals is an exercise in balancing regulatory compliance, tax efficiency, investor protection, and operational feasibility. These deals often involve multiple jurisdictions, requiring sophisticated legal and tax planning.

For example, an investment into an Indian company by a US private equity firm may involve holding entities in Singapore, Mauritius, or the

Netherlands due to tax treaties, regulatory advantages, or investment norms. The structure must align with India's FDI rules, sector-specific restrictions, and FEMA regulations. It must also comply with global anti-money-laundering, anti-corruption, and tax transparency standards.

Legal documentation must accommodate cross-border enforcement, dispute resolution, indemnity structures, representations and warranties, liquidation preferences, currency considerations, and tax gross-ups. Governance rights must reflect both local corporate law and the investor's control needs.

The complexity of cross-border structuring increases risk but also enables creative solutions that optimize tax, governance, and regulatory outcomes. Private equity firms rely on specialized advisors -lawyers, tax experts, regulatory consultants -to craft robust structures.

In India, the structuring landscape has evolved significantly. Regulatory reforms, tax clarity, and bilateral treaties have shaped how cross-border deals are executed. Investors must remain responsive to ongoing legislative changes that influence holding structures, capital flows, and repatriation mechanisms.

Cross-Border Value Creation: Bringing Global Capabilities to Local Companies

The most powerful impact of cross-border private equity lies not in capital deployment but in capability transfer. Global private equity firms bring knowledge, systems, talent, and strategic frameworks that can transform local companies. This cross-pollination accelerates growth, enhances competitiveness, and strengthens long-term resilience.

Value creation often takes the form of operational improvement. A global firm may introduce advanced manufacturing practices from Europe to an Indian industrial company. It may apply sophisticated analytics used in US retail businesses to a consumer company in Southeast Asia. It may help a local technology company adopt global cybersecurity standards.

Cross-border expertise also enhances strategic expansion. A private equity-backed Indian brand may explore international markets through partnerships, distributors, or acquisitions. A domestic logistics company may expand to the Middle East. A healthcare company may attract global clinical talent.

Governance uplift is one of the most significant contributions. Global investors introduce world-class governance standards -independent boards, audit committees, internal controls, ethical frameworks, reporting rigor, and compliance systems. These improvements not only reduce risk but prepare the company for future IPOs or strategic exits.

Cross-border firms also bring talent networks. They can help companies recruit global CXOs or specialized professionals. They may facilitate international leadership training, mentorship programs, and cultural integration initiatives.

In essence, cross-border private equity acts as a catalyst for globalizing local companies -transforming them from national players into international competitors.

India's Role in Global Private Equity: A High-Growth Opportunity

India has emerged as a critical destination for global private equity. The country's demographic strengths, entrepreneurial ecosystem, digital transformation, consumption growth, and regulatory reforms create a fertile environment for investment. At the same time, India offers complexities that require deep local understanding -family ownership dynamics, informal practices, regional diversity, and regulatory nuances.

Global firms have established significant presence in India, building large teams, sector expertise, and strong local partnerships. India has attracted investments across consumer, technology, healthcare, financial services, logistics, renewable energy, infrastructure, and manufacturing.

Several factors position India uniquely in the global private equity landscape.

The first is scale. India's population, urbanization, and consumption growth create opportunities unmatched in many emerging markets.

The second is digital adoption. India leads the world in digital payments, mobile penetration, and tech-enabled services.

The third is entrepreneurial vibrancy -thousands of startups, family businesses, and professionally run enterprises seeking growth capital.

The fourth is regulatory evolution -efforts to improve transparency, streamline compliance, strengthen governance, and facilitate foreign investment.

India also plays a role in global strategy for multinational portfolio companies. It serves as a manufacturing base, a technology hub, a consumer market, and an innovation center. Cross-border private equity strategies increasingly leverage India as both an investment destination and a partner market.

Yet India's complexity demands humility. Foreign investors must understand cultural norms, promoter priorities, and local business structures. Those who underestimate India's nuances often struggle. Those who embrace them succeed.

Risks Unique to Cross-Border Investing: Geopolitics, Currency, and Integration

Cross-border investing carries risks that extend beyond traditional dealmaking. Geopolitical risk is one of the most unpredictable. Trade wars, sanctions, border tensions, elections, and diplomatic shifts can alter cross-border exposure dramatically. Firms must assess geopolitical risk continuously and integrate it into deal selection, structuring, and portfolio management.

Currency risk is unavoidable. Fluctuations in exchange rates can turn a high-performing investment into a disappointing one after currency translation. Hedging strategies help, but they cannot eliminate risk entirely. Long-term investors must understand monetary policies, inflation trends, and macroeconomic forces in both home and host countries.

Integration risk emerges when cross-border acquisitions require the merging of cultures, systems, processes, and leadership teams. Integration failures can undermine value quickly. Private equity firms must plan integration carefully, respecting local culture while aligning with global standards.

Legal and regulatory risk increases with jurisdictional complexity. Changes in tax treaties, foreign investment rules, or compliance obligations can affect returns.

Despite these risks, cross-border investing remains attractive because the rewards -growth, diversification, global synergy -often outweigh the challenges for firms that manage risk effectively.

Cross-Border Exits: Selling to Global Buyers and Listing on International Markets

Exits in cross-border private equity often involve international buyers or global capital markets. Strategic buyers from the US, Europe, Japan, or China may acquire companies in India to enter the market or strengthen global portfolios. These buyers often pay premium valuations due to strategic fit.

Secondary sales to global private equity firms are increasingly common, especially as India's ecosystem matures. Many global investors view India as a long-term growth market and are willing to take over assets from earlier investors.

International IPOs, though less common, offer another pathway. Indian technology or consumer companies may list on Nasdaq or other global exchanges. Such listings demand exceptional governance, reporting, and scalability -criteria that cross-border private equity helps companies achieve.

Strong ESG alignment enhances cross-border exit potential, as global buyers increasingly scrutinize sustainability and governance.

Conclusion: Cross-Border Private Equity as the Frontier of Global Value Creation

Cross-border private equity investing embodies the future of global capital. It integrates financial analysis with geopolitical awareness, operational excellence with cultural fluency, and global expertise with local nuance. The firms that succeed in cross-border investing are those that understand not only business fundamentals but the human, cultural, regulatory, and strategic complexities of international environments.

Cross-border private equity demands humility, adaptability, and continuous learning. It requires partnership -between global teams and local experts, between investors and management, between cultures and markets. It demands rigorous governance, disciplined risk management, and sophisticated operational capability.

For India, cross-border private equity represents opportunity and responsibility. It brings global capital, global capabilities, and global expectations. It accelerates modernization and integration into the world economy. It challenges Indian companies to rise to global standards. And it positions India as one of the most dynamic centers of private capital in the world.

Ultimately, cross-border private equity investing is not about geography; it is about possibility. It reflects the belief that value can be created anywhere and that talent, ambition, and innovation transcend borders. It is an expression of private equity's highest potential -aligning capital with opportunity across the vast landscape of the global economy.

CHAPTER 16 - PRIVATE EQUITY IN INDIA: EVOLUTION, MILESTONES, AND THE MAKING OF A MODERN MARKET

Private equity in India is a story intertwined with the nation's economic transformation. It is the story of how global capital met a young, entrepreneurial nation on the cusp of reinvention; how decades of policy reform opened the door to new ownership models; how India's vast consumer base created once-in-a-generation opportunities; and how private equity firms -global and domestic -became architects of corporate modernization, governance reform, and organizational discipline. To understand the present dynamism of India's private equity market and its global standing, one must first understand the long arc of evolution that brought it here.

The rise of private equity in India cannot be separated from the larger narrative of India's liberalization. Before 1991, India was largely a closed, state-controlled economy. Capital flows were restricted, private enterprise was constrained, and foreign investment was minimal. Promoter-driven companies dominated the corporate landscape, often operating with informal systems, limited governance structures, and constrained access to capital. Growth was incremental and heavily regulated.

The liberalization reforms of 1991 marked a dramatic shift. The government dismantled industrial licensing, opened the economy to global competition, invited foreign capital, and introduced far-reaching changes in trade policy, financial regulation, and taxation. These reforms laid the foundation for private capital to enter India -not only in the form of foreign direct investment and public market flows, but eventually through venture capital and private equity.

The earliest wave of private equity investing in India arrived in the mid-1990s, largely through development finance institutions, sovereign-backed funds, and multilateral agencies. Their focus was on long-term growth, infrastructure, and industrial expansion. It was not until the mid-2000s, however, that private equity truly took shape as a competitive, sophisticated asset class. The convergence of economic expansion, improving regulatory frameworks, rising entrepreneurship, and global liquidity catalyzed a new era in which India became a core destination for global private equity firms.

This chapter traces that journey -from India's pre-liberalization roots to its post-liberalization boom, from the early players who shaped the market to the sophisticated ecosystem that exists today. It explores the evolution of deal types, sector focuses, exit markets, regulatory structures, and entrepreneurial attitudes. It examines global firms that shaped India's investment landscape, domestic funds that grew alongside them, and the pivotal role of Indian entrepreneurs and promoters. Most importantly, it analyses the unique characteristics of India's private equity market -a market where massive opportunity coexists with structural complexity, where demographics drive demand but governance shapes viability, and where global capital must adapt to local nuance.

What emerges is not simply a chronicle of investments but the story of India's economic modernity -a story in which private equity plays the role of both participant and catalyst.

The Pre-Liberalization Era: Seeds of a Capital-Scarce Economy

To appreciate the significance of India's private equity evolution, one must begin with the constraints of its earlier economic system. Before 1991, India operated under what was often called the "License Raj," a centralized regime of bureaucratic control that dictated who could operate in which industries, how much they could produce, what they could import, and at what scale they could expand.

The consequences were far-reaching. Companies struggled for expansion capital. Banks -mostly state-owned -prioritized lending to priority sectors, leaving little credit for innovation, consumer businesses, or emerging industries. Equity markets were shallow and underdeveloped. Entrepreneurs had limited access to institutional capital, technology, or global markets. Most companies operated informally, guided more by relationships than systems, and more by family control than corporate governance.

In this environment, the concept of private equity did not exist. There were no funds, no institutional investors, no frameworks for minority ownership, and no appetite among promoters to share equity with outside partners. Companies grew slowly, cautiously, and often without the discipline or scale that modern competition demands.

Yet beneath the surface, the seeds of entrepreneurship were present. India had a rich history of family-owned businesses, trading communities, and regional industrial clusters -textiles in Gujarat, automotive components in Tamil Nadu, pharmaceuticals in Maharashtra, and technology talent in Bengaluru. When liberalization arrived, these seeds blossomed into a vast landscape of entrepreneurial opportunity, creating fertile ground for private equity.

1991 and After: The Opening of the Indian Economy

The liberalization reforms enacted under Prime Minister P.V. Narasimha Rao and Finance Minister Dr. Manmohan Singh triggered a watershed moment in Indian economic history. Tariffs dropped sharply, foreign companies were invited to invest, industrial licensing was dismantled, and financial sector reforms accelerated. Foreign Institutional Investors (FIIs) were permitted to enter India's equity markets, and foreign direct investment (FDI) norms were progressively relaxed.

This reform wave transformed India in three fundamental ways.

First, it unleashed entrepreneurship. Indian businesses could now compete on global terms, import machinery freely, collaborate with multinational partners, and scale without bureaucratic obstruction. The Internet boom of the late 1990s added fuel to this entrepreneurial surge, particularly in software and IT services.

Second, it created demand for capital -more capital than banks or public markets could supply. Companies needed funds to expand capacity, upgrade technology, build brands, expand distribution, and modernize operations. India's traditional funding sources were insufficient for the rapid growth that the market was beginning to experience.

Third, it introduced India to global investors -private investors who saw in India a vast untapped market with demographic strength, entrepreneurial talent, and economic ambition. These investors brought not only capital but also new governance standards, value creation models, and global networks.

Venture capital appeared first, driven by the technology boom. Early funds focused on IT services, software exports, and early-stage startups. Private equity followed, targeting growth-stage companies across consumer, financial services, manufacturing, and healthcare.

By the early 2000s, India had become one of the most important emerging markets for global private equity.

The First Wave: Early Entrants and Early Experiments (1995–2005)

The earliest private equity activity in India was led by development finance institutions, such as the International Finance Corporation (IFC), CDC Group (now British International Investment), DEG, and ADB. These institutions focused on infrastructure, manufacturing, and industrial capacity building. Their investments emphasized governance, sustainability, and long-term growth.

Around the same time, global venture capital firms entered India to tap into the burgeoning IT and outsourcing sectors. Funds such as Warburg Pincus, General Atlantic, ChrysCapital, Temasek, and Sequoia Capital established operations in India. This period saw investments in software services companies such as Wipro, Infosys, and later in technology-enabled businesses.

These early firms shaped the fundamental playbook for private equity in India: a focus on growth capital, minority stakes, and partnerships with promoter-led companies. India's market dynamics differed from leveraged buyout (LBO) markets in the West. Debt markets in India were not deep enough to support aggressive leverage. Promoters were reluctant to cede control. As a result, the Indian private equity model evolved as a minority-investment ecosystem oriented around growth rather than buyouts.

This distinct model -growth equity with operational partnership -became the defining characteristic of India's private equity industry.

The Boom Years: Rapid Expansion and the Rise of Indian PE (2005–2010)

Between 2005 and 2010, India witnessed rapid economic growth, consumer expansion, and sectoral diversification. GDP growth accelerated, IT exports soared, consumption deepened, and financial inclusion improved. This was the period when private equity capital poured into India at unprecedented scale.

Global megafunds -KKR, Blackstone, Carlyle, TPG, Bain Capital, Advent International -established or expanded their India presence. Domestic funds such as ICICI Venture, Kotak PE, TVS Capital, Multiples, and True North emerged as important players. Sovereign wealth funds from Singapore, Abu Dhabi, Norway, and Canada became active investors, often bypassing traditional GPs and pursuing direct deals.

This period marked the arrival of thematic investing in India. Investors focused on sectors with structural tailwinds -consumer brands, retail, healthcare, IT services, infrastructure, logistics, financial services, and private education. Growth equity became the dominant investment style, reflecting India's vast consumer base and entrepreneurial dynamism.

Deals became larger and more sophisticated. Companies became more willing to partner with private equity firms. Promoters recognized the value of institutional capital not just as money but as an enabler of professionalism, governance, and long-term growth.

Yet this period also revealed structural challenges -information asymmetry, variable governance standards, lack of exit markets, and occasional promoter-investor conflict. These challenges gave rise to a more mature, selective, and disciplined private equity ecosystem in the years that followed.

Post-2010 Consolidation: Governance, Discipline, and Professionalization

After 2010, the private equity industry in India entered a period of consolidation and maturation. The exuberance of the previous years gave way to a sharper focus on governance, operational value creation, and disciplined underwriting.

Several factors drove this shift.

First, the global financial crisis revealed vulnerabilities in rapid-growth markets. Investors became more cautious, emphasizing cash flows, governance, and operating performance.

Second, India itself faced macroeconomic challenges during the early 2010s -slower growth, fiscal pressures, currency volatility, and inflation. Investors realized that India required local expertise, not generic emerging-market capital.

Third, many early investments struggled due to poor governance, promoter disputes, or unrealistic expectations. The industry recognized the importance of alignment, transparency, and board oversight.

Fourth, regulatory reforms strengthened investor rights. SEBI enhanced disclosure norms. RBI refined FDI and FPI frameworks. The Companies Act of 2013 mandated independent directors, audit rigor, and formal governance structures. The Insolvency and Bankruptcy Code (IBC) transformed creditor rights.

These reforms professionalized Indian corporate governance and reinforced the role of private equity as a catalyst for transparency and accountability.

2015 Onward: The Golden Age of Indian Private Equity

The period from 2015 onward represents the golden age of Indian private equity -a period marked by unprecedented capital inflows, deeper sector specialization, global-scale exits, and a more sophisticated ecosystem.

India became one of the largest private equity destinations in Asia. Global capital accelerated investments in technology, fintech, consumer brands, enterprise software, healthcare, education, real estate, and renewable energy. India produced thousands of startups, dozens of unicorns, and several world-class companies backed by private equity.

Exits matured as well. Trade sales, IPOs, secondary sales, and promoter buybacks became more common. Flipkart's acquisition by Walmart created one of the largest exits in Indian private equity history. Many funds delivered multi-billion-dollar distributions to LPs.

India's credit markets deepened, enabling more structured deals, buyouts, and platform-building strategies. The emergence of alternative investment funds (AIFs), REITs, and InvITs broadened the investment landscape.

Private equity became mainstream, not just in financial circles but in the broader business culture. Promoters increasingly welcomed private equity partners. Employees recognized private equity-backed companies as desirable workplaces. Consumers interacted daily with companies funded by private capital.

Private equity became a pillar of India's economic strategy and a key driver of modernization.

The India Model: A Distinctive Approach to Private Equity

India does not follow the classic buyout-driven model of Western private equity. Instead, it follows a unique "India model" shaped by local constraints and opportunities.

This model is defined by several distinct characteristics:

Minority investing as the norm: Most Indian promoters prefer to retain control, requiring private equity firms to master minority protection, alignment, and governance negotiation.

Growth equity more than leverage: Debt markets in India support only modest leverage, so private equity emphasizes growth, operational improvement, and strategic expansion.

Promoter-driven businesses: Investors must collaborate with founders and family owners, navigating dynamics of trust, emotion, and legacy.

Governance reform: Private equity plays an outsized role in introducing governance standards, financial discipline, and long-term thinking.

Sector specialization: India's large, diverse economy necessitates deep sector expertise -technology, healthcare, consumer, and financial services each require specialized knowledge.

Longer holding periods: Building value in India often takes time due to structural constraints and market complexity.

Deep local adaptation: Foreign investors must understand India's cultural, regulatory, linguistic, and regional diversity to succeed.

The "India model" has become a benchmark for investing in complex, high-growth emerging markets globally.

Regulation and Policy: The Framework That Shapes Investment

India's regulatory environment plays a decisive role in shaping private equity behavior. SEBI, RBI, IRDAI, MCA, and other regulatory bodies collectively define the parameters of investment, governance, and exits.

SEBI's Alternative Investment Fund (AIF) regulations established a formal structure for private equity funds, creating clear categories for venture, private equity, and credit strategies. RBI's foreign investment guidelines define sectoral caps, approval routes, pricing norms, and repatriation rules. The Companies Act dictates governance standards, board composition, and reporting obligations.

India's tax system underwent major reforms, including GAAR, BEPS compliance, GST, and treaty renegotiations. These changes created stability and transparency but required investors to adapt structures and strategies.

Infrastructure reforms such as IBC strengthened creditor rights, enabling private equity participation in distressed assets.

Regulation in India is complex but increasingly predictable -a critical factor in attracting long-term global capital.

Promoters and Private Equity: A Unique Relationship

The relationship between promoters and private equity firms is central to India's investment landscape. India's corporate sector has deep roots in family ownership, where decision-making is centralized, loyalty is prized, and informal networks govern operations. Private equity, with its emphasis on governance, transparency, and performance metrics, introduces a new cultural dynamic.

Partnership between promoters and investors requires mutual trust. Promoters often seek capital for expansion, professionalization, or succession planning. Private equity firms offer not just funds but operational expertise, governance systems, and strategic guidance. When alignment is strong, the partnership creates extraordinary value. When misaligned, it creates conflict.

Successful private equity firms in India excel at managing promoter dynamics -balancing influence with respect, enforcing governance without rigidity, and fostering collaboration rather than confrontation.

Sectors That Shaped India's Private Equity Landscape

Several sectors have played outsized roles in India's private equity growth.

Technology and SaaS transformed India into a global innovation hub. Investors supported IT services, product companies, platform businesses, and enterprise software.

Consumer and retail capitalized on rising incomes, urbanization, and brand aspiration.

Financial services and fintech became a major focus due to India's massive population, underpenetrated credit markets, and digital infrastructure.

Healthcare attracted investment due to demand growth, clinical talent, and regulatory reforms.

Infrastructure and renewable energy grew rapidly, benefiting from government incentives and global climate capital.

These sectors created category leaders that attracted global buyers, strengthened exit markets, and elevated India's position in global private equity.

India's Exit Evolution: From Scarcity to Sophistication

In the early years, exits were sporadic and difficult. Limited public market depth, promoter reluctance, and weak secondary markets created bottlenecks. Over time, India's exit ecosystem transformed dramatically.

Trade sales to global and domestic strategics became common. Secondary sales to private equity funds grew significantly. IPO markets expanded. Promoter buybacks emerged as a viable option. Structurally, exits became smoother, faster, and more competitive.

The result was a virtuous cycle -better exits attracted more capital, which enabled better companies to grow, which in turn fuelled more successful exits.

India Today: A Global Private Equity Powerhouse

India stands today as one of the world's most important markets for private equity. Its demographic dividend, entrepreneurial energy, digital infrastructure, regulatory reform, and economic resilience create unmatched long-term potential. India's private equity ecosystem includes global giants, homegrown leaders, sector specialists, sovereign funds, pension funds, venture investors, and acceleration platforms.

Promoters increasingly welcome PE capital as a partner in scale. Employees seek careers in PE-backed companies. Public markets reward companies with strong governance. Customers interact daily with brands shaped by private capital.

India's private equity ecosystem is no longer emerging -it is established, sophisticated, and influential.

Conclusion: Private Equity as a Force for India's Future

Private equity has become an integral pillar of India's economic development. It has funded growth, strengthened governance, professionalized companies, created jobs, and built enduring institutions. It has transformed startups into global contenders, family businesses into professional corporations, and informal enterprises into modern organizations.

The story of private equity in India is the story of India's ambition -its ability to adapt, innovate, collaborate, and aspire. As India enters the next phase of its economic journey, private equity will play an even more central role, aligning global capital with India's vast potential, and shaping a future defined by resilience, innovation, and sustainable growth.

CHAPTER 17 - CASE STUDIES IN INDIAN PRIVATE EQUITY

Private equity, at its core, is a business of stories. Every investment is a story about ambition and discipline, opportunity and risk, vision and execution. Some stories end in remarkable success -category leaders built from scratch, family businesses transformed into professionally governed institutions, companies strengthened through operational rigor and strategic clarity. Others reveal the difficulties of investing in a market as complex and textured as India -governance conflicts, market disruptions, overestimations of scale, or the delicate dance between promoters and investors.

In India, private equity's role as an agent of transformation is particularly visible. The companies that have shaped modern Indian consumer behavior, digital infrastructure, logistics networks, healthcare systems, and financial inclusion often carry the fingerprints of private capital. Yet each success or failure is the result of thousands of choices -by founders, fund managers, boards, customers, regulators, and markets. These stories are windows into the craft of private equity in India.

This chapter presents deeply detailed case studies of Indian private equity -told not as bullet points or clinical after-action reports but as unfolding narratives. Each story illustrates a different facet of the Indian market: the complexities of partnering with founders, the discipline of scaling businesses, the role of governance, the challenges of hypergrowth, the use of sectoral expertise, the mechanics of exits, and the fragile balance between ambition and reality.

The stories included here are not celebratory monologues; they are analytical narratives -honest, nuanced, and reflective. They show how private equity firms respond to uncertainty, negotiate alignment, and remain anchored in fundamentals even as markets oscillate between exuberance and correction.

Case Study 1: Flipkart - The Deal That Redefined Indian Private Equity

From Startup Gamble to India's Largest-Ever Exit

When private equity and venture investors first met Sachin and Binny Bansal in the late 2000s, India's e-commerce landscape was barely recognizable. Internet penetration was low, digital payments were unreliable, logistics networks were fragmented, and consumer trust in online buying was fragile. Building a large online marketplace in India seemed, to many, a distant dream. But the Bansals had a conviction that India's digital consumer was merely waiting for a catalyst.

Early investors like Accel and Tiger Global backed the founders long before e-commerce became fashionable. These early decisions required extraordinary imagination: investors bet not only on a company but on the creation of an entirely new category.

As Flipkart expanded, the business consumed capital at breathtaking speed. Growth demanded warehouses, technology, delivery networks, customer education, and deep discounting. Private equity investors -Tiger Global, Naspers, SoftBank, and others -infused billions into Flipkart over the years. Their role extended far beyond capital. They helped design governance structures, enforce financial discipline, hire global executives, and push the company toward professionalized operations.

The transformation from founder-led startup to institutionally governed corporation was not easy. There were disagreements on strategy, burn rates, leadership transitions, and competitive responses to Amazon's entry into India. At times the company wavered under pressure -unit economics were volatile, logistics strained, and customer acquisition costs soared. But private equity investors pushed for operational discipline: reducing inefficiencies, prioritizing high-frequency categories, and building proprietary supply chain infrastructure.

The exit was historic. In 2018, Walmart acquired 77% of Flipkart for approximately $16 billion -creating one of the largest exits in global private equity. Tiger Global alone generated billions in returns. The deal proved that Indian companies could attract the world's largest strategic buyers, and that private equity could build category-defining businesses at global scale.

Flipkart's story became a symbol of Indian private equity's maturation: the willingness to take bold bets, the patience to endure years of losses, the discipline to professionalize operations, and the resilience required to navigate ferocious competition.

Case Study 2: ChrysCapital and Mankind Pharma - The Art of Long-Term, Disciplined Investing

The story of ChrysCapital's investment in Mankind Pharma is one of the most celebrated examples of classical, fundamentals-driven private equity in India. It is a study in diligence, alignment, operational partnership, and disciplined value creation -and perhaps the finest illustration of how private equity works best in India.

When ChrysCapital first evaluated Mankind, the company was already known within the pharmaceutical industry as a fast-growing, unconventional player. Its focus on affordable drugs, deep reach into Tier-2 and Tier-3 towns, and no-frills marketing approach differentiated it from traditional pharma giants. Many investors dismissed Mankind as too unorthodox, too rural, too dependent on aggressive front-line execution.

But ChrysCapital saw a different story. The firm recognized that Mankind had a cost structure advantage, a deep understanding of India's middle-and lower-income markets, and an operational model that could scale with the right governance. After extensive diligence -including field visits with medical representatives and detailed analysis of SKU-level economics -ChrysCapital made its investment.

The partnership between ChrysCapital and the Juneja family (Mankind's promoters) exemplified how alignment can drive exceptional outcomes. ChrysCapital introduced governance systems, strengthened financial reporting, assisted with strategic planning, and professionalized senior leadership. Yet it respected the promoter's expertise in distribution, pricing, and brand building.

Over the years, Mankind transformed into one of India's most successful pharmaceutical companies. ChrysCapital exited with extraordinary returns -reportedly over 20x -making it one of the most profitable private equity deals in Indian history.

This case underscores the strengths of Indian private equity when executed with discipline: deep diligence, promoter alignment, operational support, and patience.

Case Study 3: Global Infrastructure Partners in Adani Transmission - A Study in Large-Scale Platform Investing

Infrastructure in India is a story of chronic deficit and perpetual opportunity. Global Infrastructure Partners (GIP) recognized this early, entering a sector rife with complexities -regulatory hurdles, capital intensity, construction delays, and political risk. Yet these complexities also created barriers to entry, making infrastructure a fertile ground for specialized investors.

GIP's investment in Adani Transmission was emblematic of its approach. The company sat at the intersection of India's energy transformation: rising demand, regulatory reforms, and the shift toward renewable energy. Transmission, though less glamorous than generation, offered long-term contracted cash flows and clear regulatory frameworks.

The investment required deep technical diligence: reviewing asset quality, regulatory filings, tariff structures, concession agreements, and long-term demand projections. GIP also evaluated the Adani Group's governance systems, financing discipline, and operational track record.

Post-investment, GIP played a strategic role in strengthening the platform -supporting acquisitions, streamlining processes, and helping the company raise global capital. The investment demonstrated how private equity could play in sectors traditionally dominated by government or local conglomerates.

This case highlighted the increasing sophistication of India's infrastructure landscape -where global funds deploy billions into long-duration assets requiring analytical rigor and geopolitical awareness.

Case Study 4: TPG and Manipal Hospitals - Scaling Healthcare with Discipline and Purpose

Healthcare in India has long faced the dual challenge of scale and quality. Operating hospitals requires medical expertise, governance discipline, patient-centric culture, and capital efficiency. Many hospital chains struggled to balance expansion with clinical excellence.

TPG's investment in Manipal Hospitals showed how private equity can navigate this delicate balance. When TPG partnered with the Pai family, Manipal was a respected but regionally concentrated healthcare provider. It had strong clinical reputation but limited national presence.

TPG saw an opportunity to professionalize the organization, expand its footprint, and build one of India's most trusted hospital chains. The fund worked closely with management to standardize clinical protocols, strengthen governance, optimize asset utilization, and expand through targeted acquisitions.

Healthcare diligence is among the most complex in private equity -requiring evaluation of patient outcomes, doctor relationships, local regulatory compliance, medical equipment, and specialty mix. TPG invested heavily in understanding each clinical vertical, ensuring that expansion did not come at the cost of quality.

The partnership culminated in Manipal acquiring Columbia Asia and Vikram Hospitals, transforming it into one of India's largest healthcare networks. TPG eventually executed a high-value secondary sale, reinforcing its reputation as a disciplined healthcare investor.

This case became a benchmark for how private equity can build institutional-grade healthcare systems in emerging markets.

Case Study 5: The Zomato–Info Edge–Ant Financial Arc - The Evolution of India's Consumer Internet Investing

Zomato's story captures the evolution of Indian consumer internet -from fledgling startup to global tech contender. Info Edge, one of India's earliest and most successful internet-era investors, provided Zomato with not just capital but a strategic cushion that allowed experimentation and adaptation.

Over time, investors like Sequoia and Ant Financial enabled Zomato to scale aggressively -expanding into new categories, entering international markets, and building last-mile delivery capabilities.

Private equity played a key role in navigating Zomato's complex hypergrowth phase -encouraging discipline, capital allocation, and governance modernization.

Zomato became one of the first Indian startups to successfully list on public markets, paving the way for a new era of private equity-to-IPO exits. The company's journey highlighted the challenges of scaling a network-driven business -balancing burn rates, defending against competition, and transforming from founder-centric culture to institutional governance.

The Zomato case showcased the unique interplay between venture, growth equity, and crossover investors in India's tech ecosystem.

Case Study 6: A Failure - The Cautionary Tale of a High-Growth Retail Chain (Name Withheld)

When Alignment Breaks and Expansion Outpaces Discipline

Not all private equity stories in India end with triumph. Some offer sobering lessons about governance breakdowns, misaligned incentives, unrealistic growth assumptions, or failure to adapt.

One mid-market retail chain -whose name we will not cite out of sensitivity -provides such a lesson. The company showed early promise: strong brand resonance, a charismatic founder, and rapid store expansion across India. A prominent private equity fund invested at a time when organized retail was booming, confident that India's consumption story would propel the business to scale.

But beneath the surface, the company suffered from structural weaknesses. Expansion was too fast, inventory cycles too inefficient, and store economics uneven across regions. Governance systems were weak, financial reporting inconsistent, and decision-making overly centralized around the founder.

Private equity investors attempted course correction -reducing expansion, strengthening internal controls, hiring experienced retail professionals, and renegotiating leases. Yet management resisted, viewing investor involvement as interference. The board lacked independence, and strategic disagreements intensified.

When economic slowdown struck, the company struggled. Stores underperformed, debt increased, and capital dried up. Private equity ultimately wrote down its investment substantially.

This case highlighted a fundamental truth: in India's private equity ecosystem, alignment with promoters and governance discipline are not optional -they are existential.

Conclusion: Case Studies as Mirrors of a Complex Market

Each story in this chapter illuminates a different truth about private equity in India. Flipkart demonstrates the audacity required to back category-defining founders. Mankind Pharma shows the power of fundamentals-driven investing. Manipal Hospitals reveals the nuance of operational value creation in regulated sectors. Cross-border investments like Adani Transmission highlight the role of global capital in modernizing India's infrastructure. Zomato illustrates the evolution of tech investing. And the unnamed retail chain exposes the pitfalls of poor governance and misalignment.

Taken together, these stories show that private equity in India is not a monolithic discipline. It is a mosaic of strategies, relationships, risks, and outcomes. It rewards deep insight, patience, and discipline. It punishes superficiality, complacency, and misalignment. It thrives when investors respect India's cultural, regulatory, and business complexities -and when they combine global standards with local nuance.

Private equity in India is still young relative to Western markets, but its stories are rich, instructive, and increasingly global in impact. These case studies form the narrative backbone of an industry that is shaping India's economic future.

CHAPTER 18 -THE FUTURE OF PRIVATE EQUITY: TECHNOLOGY, CLIMATE, SOCIETY, AND THE NEXT FRONTIER OF VALUE CREATION

Private equity is often described as an industry built on financial discipline, strategic clarity, and operational excellence. Yet beneath its analytical rigor lies a deeper truth: private equity is fundamentally an industry shaped by change. Every investment opportunity is born from some form of disruption -technological, demographic, regulatory, geopolitical, or behavioral. The most successful investors are those who anticipate change before it becomes visible in financial statements, who interpret shifts in human behavior before they appear in macro indicators, and who position their portfolios not merely to withstand disruption but to benefit from it.

Over the past three decades, private equity has already undergone dramatic transformation. It evolved from leveraged buyouts in the 1980s to global growth capital in the 2000s, from financial engineering in the 1990s to operational value creation in the 2010s, and from generalist investing to sector specialization in the 2020s. Yet the changes of the next twenty years will dwarf those of the past. Technology -particularly artificial intelligence -will redefine how deals are sourced, evaluated, executed, and monitored. Climate change will alter capital flows, reshape industries, and create new sectors of investment altogether. Demographic shifts will transform consumption, labor markets, healthcare demands, and urban development. Regulation will adapt to new realities, from data privacy to sustainability reporting to geopolitics. And global capital will become more fluid, more transparent, and more democratically accessible.

This chapter examines these forces not as abstract trends but as concrete trajectories that will determine the future landscape of private equity. It asks fundamental questions: How will artificial intelligence change the nature of investment judgment? Will climate risk become the dominant factor in valuation? How will sovereign wealth funds redefine the balance of global capital? Will private equity become more democratized, accessible not only to institutions but to individuals? Will emerging markets like India become core engines of global returns? What will happen to traditional buyout strategies in a world of intangible assets, platform economies, and nonlinear growth?

These questions invite exploration not only of financial theory but of sociology, technology, geopolitics, and ethics. Private equity does not exist in a vacuum. It is shaped by the world around it -and by the world it helps shape.

The First Great Transformation: Artificial Intelligence and the Analytical Revolution

Artificial intelligence is not simply another technological tool; it represents a fundamental transformation in how information is processed, decisions are made, and organizations operate. Just as spreadsheets revolutionized finance in the 1980s and the Internet redefined business models in the 2000s, AI will reshape private equity at every stage of the investment lifecycle.

Artificial intelligence will change how deals are sourced. Today, sourcing remains a relationship-driven activity, heavily dependent on networks, founder interactions, bankers, and sector familiarity. But as AI systems gain the ability to scan large volumes of unstructured data -industry filings, job postings, satellite imagery, search trends, e-commerce reviews, logistics records, financial statements, social signals -a new paradigm emerges. AI will identify patterns that humans cannot: emerging categories before they mature, shifting consumer tastes before they become mainstream, operational anomalies before they become problems. Deal sourcing will shift from reactive to anticipatory.

Diligence will become far more precise. AI systems will evaluate customer behavior, supply chain risk, pricing elasticity, churn patterns, seasonality, and operational efficiency with unprecedented granularity. Instead of relying on weeks of interviews and manual analysis, investors will access real-time insight into how a company is performing and where its blind spots lie. Yet diligence will not become fully automated. It will require new forms of judgment -interpreting machine-generated insights, challenging algorithmic bias, and understanding when human intuition must override statistical probability.

AI will also reshape value creation. Operating partners will use predictive analytics to optimize pricing, personalize customer interactions, monitor supply chains, forecast failures in manufacturing equipment, or detect unusual behavioral patterns in employee or customer activity. AI-enabled automation will transform organizational design, allowing portfolio companies to scale without proportional headcount growth. Entire industries will reorganize around AI -from healthcare diagnostics to industrial maintenance, from financial underwriting to logistics optimization.

Private equity firms themselves will change. Analysts and associates will spend less time on manual modelling or data cleaning and more time on strategic thinking, pattern recognition, and human decision-making. Partners will become curators of AI-augmented insight. The firms that thrive will be those that combine technological sophistication with the timeless essentials of investing: judgment, discipline, humility, and the ability to build trust with founders and management teams.

Ultimately, AI will not replace investors; it will amplify them. But it will also widen the gap between firms that embrace technology and those that cling to traditional processes.

The Second Great Transformation: Climate, Sustainability, and the Reordering of Global Capital

Climate change represents the single largest structural force reshaping global industry. It will affect every sector -energy, agriculture, transportation, real estate, finance, manufacturing, and consumer products. Private equity, as an allocator of long-term capital, will play a pivotal role in the transition to a low-carbon economy.

Climate risk will become central to investment underwriting. Extreme weather events, water scarcity, regulatory pressure, carbon pricing, supply chain vulnerabilities, and shifting consumer preferences will redefine business viability. Companies that ignore environmental risk will face rising costs, shrinking customer bases, and degraded valuations. Conversely, companies that adapt early -through energy efficiency, circular supply chains, sustainable product design, and climate-resilient operations -will benefit from regulatory incentives, cost savings, and brand differentiation.

Entirely new sectors will emerge. Renewable energy will continue to attract capital, but the growth frontier will extend to battery storage, carbon capture, green hydrogen, climate adaptation technologies, electric mobility ecosystems, smart grids, sustainable agriculture, waste-to-energy systems, and water management. Private equity firms with deep sector specialization will dominate these areas, much as specialized energy investors dominated the shale boom in the United States.

ESG, once considered a soft discipline, will evolve into a rigorous, data-driven model of risk-adjusted investing. Environmental metrics will become standardized. Companies will be evaluated based on emissions intensity, energy mix, water efficiency, biodiversity impact, and supply chain transparency. Sustainability reporting will become mandatory in most major economies, making ESG not a voluntary exercise but a regulatory requirement.

One of the most profound shifts will be the rise of climate-aligned capital pools. Sovereign funds, pension funds, and endowments will direct capital toward sustainable investments not only out of moral imperative but because climate-resilient assets offer superior long-term risk profiles. Private equity firms that cannot articulate credible climate strategies will find themselves excluded from these capital pools. Those who build expertise in climate-aligned investing will gain a structural edge.

The future of private equity will therefore be inseparable from the future of the planet.

The Third Great Transformation: The Changing Geography of Global Returns

Over the next two decades, the geography of private equity returns will shift. Developed markets will continue to attract massive capital, but their growth will be constrained by demographic aging, lower productivity growth, and market saturation. In contrast, emerging markets -particularly India -will become central engines of global private equity returns.

India will play a pivotal role for several reasons. Its demographic profile is uniquely favorable, with a young population entering the workforce at a scale unmatched by any major economy except possibly parts of Africa. India's digital infrastructure -from Aadhaar to UPI -creates frictionless environments for financial inclusion, commerce, and innovation. Its entrepreneurial ecosystem is vibrant, producing thousands of startups and a growing number of globally competitive technology firms. Its consumption economy is expanding rapidly, driven by rising income, urbanization, and aspirational behavior.

Private equity capital will increasingly flow toward markets where consumption, digital adoption, climate innovation, and formalization converge. India becomes the archetype of such a market: massive, dynamic, complex, and open to global capital.

Other regions will also emerge. Southeast Asia will see rising inflows as economies like Indonesia, Vietnam, and the Philippines mature. Africa will present long-term potential driven by demographics and natural resources, though infrastructural gaps and governance risks will limit short-term deployment. Latin America will see cycles of opportunity tied to political shifts and commodity markets.

Global firms will reorganize around this new map. They will allocate more resources to Asia, build on-the-ground sector expertise, and adapt to local complexities. Domestic funds in these markets will also rise -offering deep local insight, faster decision-making, and relationships that global firms may struggle to replicate.

The future of private equity will therefore be multipolar, not Western-centric. India will be one of the world's main gravitational centers for private capital.

The Fourth Great Transformation: The Democratization of Private Markets

For most of its history, private equity has been accessible only to large institutions and ultra-high-net-worth individuals. But this exclusivity is beginning to change. Regulators, technology platforms, and asset managers are exploring ways to democratize private markets -allowing sophisticated retail investors to participate in categories previously reserved for institutions.

Several forces are converging. Digital investment platforms are enabling fractional ownership of private equity funds. Tokenization -using blockchain to represent ownership in funds or assets -may make private market exposure liquid, transparent, and portable. Pension funds and insurance companies are increasing allocations to private equity, indirectly exposing millions of individuals to the asset class. Meanwhile, regulatory frameworks in the United States, Europe, and Asia are evolving to permit "semi-liquid" private equity funds accessible to affluent individuals.

This democratization will alter private equity's structure. Firms will need to communicate more transparently, report more frequently, and adopt more standardized practices. Fund structures may evolve toward hybrid liquidity models. Technology will enable individuals to access curated, diversified private market portfolios.

Yet democratization will also require caution. Private equity is complex, illiquid, and long-term. Retail investors must be protected through meaningful regulation and education. The industry will need to balance accessibility with responsibility.

Nevertheless, the long-term trajectory is clear: private equity will no longer be confined to elite institutions. It will become a mainstream component of global retirement and wealth management systems.

The Fifth Great Transformation: Geopolitics and the Fragmentation of Globalization

Geopolitics will play a defining role in the future of private equity. For decades, global capitalism operated on the assumption of broad geopolitical stability. Capital flowed freely across borders. Supply chains spanned continents. Regulatory systems converged. Investors operated with confidence that the world would remain integrated.

That assumption is fading. Geopolitical tensions -between the United States and China, between Europe and Russia, across the Middle East, within Asia -have begun to reshape global markets. Protectionism is rising. Supply chains are shifting toward resilience and regionalization. Data privacy and national security concerns are influencing investment decisions.

Private equity firms will need to navigate this increasingly fragmented world. Cross-border deals will require deeper geopolitical diligence. Technology investments will be influenced by national security restrictions. Companies with international supply chains must consider political risk alongside cost efficiency. Investors must anticipate regulatory shifts, sanctions regimes, and trade realignments.

At the same time, geopolitical fragmentation will create opportunity. Countries seeking strategic independence will invest heavily in domestic manufacturing, energy independence, digital infrastructure, and defense ecosystems. Private equity firms positioned to support these national initiatives will benefit.

The future global landscape will not be defined by seamless globalization but by strategic regionalization -and private equity will need to adapt its investment playbook accordingly.

The Sixth Great Transformation: The Changing Nature of Assets and the End of Tangibility

Historically, private equity focused on tangible businesses -manufacturing plants, retail chains, physical infrastructure, and traditional industries. But today, the world's most valuable companies derive their worth from intangible assets: intellectual property, brand equity, network effects, data, algorithms, content, and communities.

This shift poses new challenges for private equity. Traditional due diligence frameworks -based on physical assets, cash flow history, and cost structures -must be reengineered to evaluate intangible drivers such as platform engagement, customer cohorts, data defensibility, and product stickiness. Valuation models must incorporate non-linear growth patterns and winner-takes-most economics.

Operational value creation must also adapt. Investors need expertise in data governance, product roadmaps, engineering culture, cybersecurity, digital marketing, and ecosystem strategy. Talent becomes the central asset -more valuable than machinery or real estate. Retention, culture, and organizational design become core parts of value creation plans.

As artificial intelligence accelerates this shift, intangible assets will dominate even further. Companies will differentiate through proprietary datasets, machine learning models, and digital distribution. Private equity firms must develop the ability to evaluate and scale these assets, not just manage cost structures.

This marks the end of an era when physical scale was the primary driver of competitive advantage. The future belongs to intangible scale -and to the investors who understand it.

The Seventh Great Transformation: Human Capital, Leadership, and the Psychology of Organizations

As businesses become more complex, one of the most critical determinants of private equity success will be the quality of leadership within portfolio companies. The future will place unprecedented demands on CEOs and management teams. They will need to navigate digital disruption, geopolitical uncertainty, regulatory scrutiny, climate risks, and workforce evolution -all while maintaining financial performance and organizational coherence.

Private equity firms will increasingly invest in leadership development: coaching, succession planning, cultural transformation, and organizational design. Emotional intelligence will matter as much as analytical precision. Boards will require deeper diversity -not only demographic but cognitive and experiential. Teams will need the ability to operate across cultures and time zones.

Remote work, hybrid models, and global talent marketplaces will redefine labor economics. Companies will need to win the war for talent not through compensation alone but through culture, purpose, learning, and flexibility.

Private equity's greatest challenge -and opportunity -will lie in shaping human organizations capable of thriving amidst complexity. This requires not only capital but insight into the psychology of leadership and the sociology of teams.

Serial Transformation: A World Where Change Never Ends

In previous decades, companies could obtain competitive advantage through a single major transformation -ERP implementation, geographic expansion, cost restructuring, or brand repositioning. But in the coming decades, competitive advantage will require continuous transformation. Markets will evolve faster than companies can ossify. Business models will need reinvention every few years. Operational excellence will require constant recalibration. Talent models will shift continuously.

Private equity firms will become architects of serial transformation. They will need to guide companies through constant reinvention

-product evolution, digital adoption, climate adaptation, regulatory compliance, organizational redesign, and global expansion.

This will create new models of ownership. Continuation funds, for example, will allow investors to hold companies for 10–15 years, driving multiple waves of improvement. Flexible capital structures will allow investors to pivot across equity, credit, and hybrid instruments. Multi-platform private equity firms will operate like diversified strategics -combining buyout, growth, venture, infrastructure, credit, and climate strategies.

The future will not favor static investors. It will favor adaptive architects.

Conclusion: Private Equity's Next Era -A Discipline Expanded, Not Transformed

Private equity will change profoundly over the next two decades, but its core will remain the same: judgment, discipline, alignment, and long-term ownership. Technology will amplify analysis, but judgment will remain a human art. Climate will reshape industries, but disciplined underwriting will remain essential. Globalization will evolve into regionalization, but the search for growth will continue. Capital will democratize, but stewardship will remain a responsibility. Company structures will change, but value will still be created by people -founders, CEOs, employees, and investors -who understand each other and share a vision.

The future of private equity is not a departure from the past but an expansion of it -a broadening of the definition of value, a deepening of the meaning of stewardship, and a widening of the horizons of opportunity. Private equity will play a central role in shaping the next phase of global economic development, including India's rise as a global economic powerhouse.

The next era belongs to the investors and firms that can combine technology with wisdom, capital with responsibility, and global insight with local nuance. The future of private equity is vast, complex, and full of possibility -and those who embrace its complexity will define the next generation of global value creation.

CHAPTER 19 -THE LP PERSPECTIVE: HOW INSTITUTIONAL INVESTORS EVALUATE PRIVATE EQUITY FUNDS

Private equity firms are often celebrated as the protagonists of the investment world -bold decision-makers, deal architects, builders of companies, stewards of transformation. But behind every private equity deal, behind every fund raised, behind every exit celebrated, stands a quieter, less visible force: the limited partners. These institutions -pension funds, sovereign wealth funds, endowments, insurance companies, family offices, and development finance institutions -are the true architects of global private equity. They supply the capital that powers the industry, they define its incentives, they shape its evolution, and through their allocation choices they ultimately determine which firms rise and which fade.

To understand private equity deeply, one must understand how LPs think. They operate with longer time horizons, broader mandates, and more complex governance structures than the funds they invest in. They must satisfy their own stakeholders -retirees, students, citizens, policy-makers, or philanthropies -while navigating an increasingly complex global financial environment. LPs do not chase deals; they evaluate managers. They do not compete for control; they compete for insight. Their discipline is different, but no less sophisticated.

This chapter provides a rare inside look into the world of LPs: how they evaluate fund managers, how they construct portfolios, how they assess risk and discipline, how they negotiate terms, and how they monitor performance over decades. It explores not only the analytical frameworks LPs use but also the cultural, organizational, and psychological dynamics that define their work. It examines how LP expectations have evolved -from early-stage trust-based commitments to today's rigorous due diligence, ESG scrutiny, and performance benchmarking. And it connects these dynamics to the Indian market, where global LPs are increasingly allocating large pools of capital with high expectations of governance, consistency, and maturity.

The story of private equity is incomplete without the story of LPs -because without them, the entire system would collapse.

The Institutional Mindset: Investing for Generations, Not Quarters

The first defining characteristic of LP thinking is the nature of their mandate. A pension fund or sovereign wealth fund does not invest for the next five years; it invests for the next fifty. Its obligations stretch far beyond the lives of its current staff and management. A pension fund must ensure that teachers, nurses, firefighters, and public-sector workers receive their benefits decades from now. A sovereign fund must steward the wealth of a nation, shielding it from economic cycles and safeguarding it for future generations. An endowment must support universities, hospitals, or research organizations in perpetuity.

This sense of intergenerational responsibility fundamentally alters how LPs approach risk, return, and alignment. Their objective is not simply to maximize return -it is to maximize *long-term risk-adjusted* return. They must avoid permanent capital loss, minimize volatility at the portfolio level, and ensure consistency of outcomes. Their evaluation horizon spans multiple economic cycles, multiple fund vintages, multiple leadership teams within both GPs and LP institutions.

Because of this, LPs view private equity through a prism of durability. They ask:

Is this manager consistent? Are their processes repeatable? Can their performance persist across cycles? Do they have succession plans? Are they capable of managing risk in good and bad markets? Are they governed responsibly? Are their incentives aligned with ours?

This long-term, risk-conscious mindset explains why LPs often invest not in the hottest managers of the moment but in those with proven discipline over decades.

The Anatomy of Manager Evaluation: What LPs Really Look For

From the outside, it may appear that LPs chase performance numbers, selecting GPs based on high returns. But insiders know that LP evaluation is far more nuanced. LPs look past the numbers to the quality of the machine that produces those numbers.

When an LP evaluates a GP, they are not merely assessing the potential future return; they are assessing *repeatability*. They want evidence that the GP's past performance is the result of process, not luck; of discipline, not momentum; of skill, not market cycles.

This evaluation unfolds across multiple dimensions:

LPs study the investment strategy -the sectors chosen, the geography, the deal size, the value creation playbook, the competitive advantage. They examine whether the strategy is coherent and whether it matches the GP's actual track record. Many GPs claim specialization, but LPs can detect whether that specialization is deep or superficial. LPs are cautious of "style drift," where a GP changes its strategy dramatically between funds, often chasing trends.

LPs also examine the team. In private equity, people *are* the product. LPs therefore focus intensely on the quality, experience, chemistry, and stability of the investment team. They ask: Who makes decisions? Who finds deals? Who creates value? Who controls exits? They analyze the division of responsibilities, the compensation structure, the decision-making hierarchy, the autonomy of junior talent, and the succession path for senior leaders.

They then scrutinize the investment process. How deals are sourced. How they are screened. How diligence is conducted. How risks are assessed. How committees operate. How value creation plans are built. How exits are anticipated. LPs frequently request sample investment memos, committee minutes, and internal reports to evaluate the GP's rigor.

Track record, of course, matters -deeply. But LPs dissect it carefully. They analyze attribution -who contributed what to performance. They examine the dispersion of returns -do a few deals drive the entire fund, or is performance broad-based? They examine consistency across vintages. They analyze how the manager performed during downturns, not just bull markets. They study unrealized value with scepticism, knowing that mark-to-model valuations can be optimistic.

They also evaluate culture. Does the firm embrace humility or arrogance? Do they learn from mistakes? Do they prioritize governance? Are they transparent or defensive? Culture, for LPs, is often the leading indicator of long-term success.

Finally, LPs evaluate alignment. Fee structures, carried interest allocations, GP commitments, internal governance -LPs want GPs whose incentives are strongly tied to fund performance, not asset accumulation.

To the untrained eye, LP evaluation can appear slow, conservative, even bureaucratic. In reality, it is one of the most intellectually rich and structurally important disciplines in finance: determining where the world's long-term capital should be entrusted.

Fundraising Dynamics: The Subtle Power of LPs

Private equity fundraising is often framed as a GP-driven process -glossy pitch decks, roadshows, and capital targets. But experienced participants know that the real power lies with the LPs. They determine which funds close quickly, which struggle, and which never make it to first close.

A typical institutional LP receives hundreds of fund pitches each year and must decide which to back based on limited bandwidth. Their evaluation window may last months or even years. Relationships matter, but relationships alone are insufficient. LPs rely on due diligence questionnaires, on-site visits, reference checks, background investigations, and deeply analytical discussions.

Global LPs, particularly the most sophisticated sovereign funds and pension plans, conduct "deep-dive diligence" that goes beyond numbers. They meet junior and mid-level staff to assess the firm's culture. They review historical committee debates to understand dissent and decision-making. They request case studies of deals that *failed*, insisting on understanding how the GP responded under stress. They evaluate ESG integration and climate considerations. They analyze portfolio construction discipline and capital pacing.

Through this process, LPs often categorize GPs into three informal tiers:

1. **"Must-have" managers** -typically oversubscribed, with LPs competing for allocation.
2. **"Considered but require diligence" managers** -where performance is strong but consistency or experience is incomplete.
3. **"Opportunistic or unproven" managers** -new funds, spinouts, or restructured teams.

LPs rarely abandon relationships easily. They invest with the same GP across multiple vintages, creating long-term partnerships. Trust, transparency, and consistency become currency.

For GPs, therefore, fundraising is not about marketing. It is about building a machine that LPs believe in.

Portfolio Construction: The Hidden Art of LP Risk Management

LPs operate massive, multi-asset portfolios spanning equities, bonds, real estate, infrastructure, hedge funds, private equity, and credit. Private equity typically occupies between 5% and 20% of their portfolio, depending on mandate and risk appetite. But constructing the private equity portion is itself an elegant balancing act.

Institutional LPs aim to create diversified private equity exposure across geography, sector, strategy, and vintage year. They allocate to buyout, growth, venture, secondaries, co-investments, and private credit. They diversify across the United States, Europe, Asia, and increasingly emerging markets. They stagger commitments across vintages to avoid concentration risk.

But LPs also manage liquidity carefully. Private equity cash flows are irregular -capital is called unpredictably, and distributions arrive in waves. LPs must forecast liquidity needs decades in advance to avoid overcommitment or shortfall.

They also monitor "denominator effects" -when public markets fall, private equity's share of the overall portfolio rises automatically, sometimes breaching allocation limits. This creates pressure to pause new commitments or rebalance exposures.

LP portfolio construction is deeply mathematical but also deeply human. It requires judgment about macro cycles, geopolitical shifts, and sector trajectories. The best LPs are not those who chase the highest-return GPs but those who create portfolios that are resilient, diversified, and strategically coherent.

Monitoring and Governance: The LP's Continuing Role

Once commitments are made, LPs continue to monitor GPs closely. They review quarterly reports, attend annual meetings, analyze underlying portfolio performance, and evaluate operational updates. They track changes in team composition, strategy drift, or portfolio company performance.

LPs also hold GPs accountable during downturns. When performance falters, LPs demand clarity, corrective action plans, and evidence of learning. When governance issues arise, LPs may push for leadership changes or internal reviews.

For global LPs, ESG monitoring has become central. They evaluate emissions, diversity metrics, compliance breaches, data privacy incidents, and sustainability initiatives across every portfolio company. They expect GPs to report transparently and to act responsibly.

Monitoring is not adversarial; it is collaborative. The best LPs treat GPs as partners but expect professionalism and consistency in return.

Co-Investments and Direct Investing: How LPs Became More Than Capital Providers

Over the past decade, many large LPs have expanded beyond fund commitments to co-investments and even direct investments. Co-investments allow LPs to deploy more capital into specific deals alongside GPs, often with lower fees. This provides LPs with more control, better visibility, and improved net returns.

Direct investing -where LPs build in-house teams that evaluate and execute deals independently -reflects the rise of "sovereign-style" asset management. Funds like Temasek, GIC, CPP Investments, and ADIA now compete with private equity firms directly, especially in large, stable companies. This shifts the power dynamic in the industry.

Yet co-investing and direct investing are not simple add-ons. They require internal expertise, governance structures, risk management frameworks, and talent. Only the most sophisticated LPs pursue them, but for those who do, the advantages are considerable: deeper control, lower costs, and stronger insight.

The Indian LP Landscape: A Market of Opportunity and Constraint

India's LP ecosystem is still young but rapidly evolving. Historically, domestic institutional investors -insurance companies, pension funds, banks -were largely absent from private equity due to regulatory barriers and conservative mandates. As a result, India relied heavily on global LPs for private market capital.

Over time, regulations have slowly shifted. Domestic pensions and insurance companies are beginning to allocate to private equity, though cautiously. The emergence of domestic AIFs has created a more formal structure for local capital participation. Family offices have become active LPs, often backing sector-specific or mid-market funds.

Global LPs, however, remain the backbone of Indian private equity. Sovereign funds from Singapore, Canada, Abu Dhabi, and Europe are among the largest investors in India. They are drawn by India's growth potential but expect governance rigor, transparency, and discipline from GPs. Their evaluation of Indian funds is often more stringent due to perceptions of governance risk and market volatility.

Indian GPs must therefore operate at global standards to attract and retain LP capital.

The Future of LP-GP Relationships: Transparency, Sustainability, and Strategic Collaboration

The relationship between LPs and GPs is evolving. In the future, LPs will demand even greater transparency -real-time reporting, granular portfolio data, ESG disclosures, climate metrics, and AI-based risk dashboards. They will expect GPs to integrate artificial intelligence into diligence, monitoring, and value creation. They will require climate strategies that go beyond compliance.

LPs will also expect GPs to demonstrate leadership in diversity, succession planning, culture, and long-term vision. Firms that fail to evolve culturally will face capital flight.

Strategic collaboration will deepen. LPs will seek more co-investments, more customized mandates, and more sector alignment. GPs will need to accommodate these requests without diluting their own investment discipline.

The LP-GP relationship will become less transactional and more partnership-driven -anchored in shared philosophy, long-term alignment, and mutual accountability.

Conclusion: LPs as the Long-Term Stewards of Global Capital

Private equity's success is built on the confidence of its limited partners -institutions that manage the hopes, savings, and futures of millions of people. LPs bring discipline to an industry prone to excitement. They reward consistency, humility, and rigor. They punish style drift, governance failure, and arrogance. They force GPs to justify their decisions not only with narrative but with evidence. They shape the culture of the industry by rewarding firms that build strong teams, invest responsibly, and manage risk intelligently.

To understand private equity, one must understand LPs -not as background players, but as the stewards of global capital whose decisions shape the very architecture of the industry. They are the anchors of discipline in a world driven by cycles of euphoria and fear. They are the unseen guardians of intergenerational responsibility. They are the ultimate judges of which investment philosophies deserve longevity.

In the long arc of private equity, LPs are not merely the providers of capital. They are the custodians of purpose, stability, and sustainability -ensuring that the industry remains not only profitable but principled.

CHAPTER 20 -THE HUMAN SIDE OF PRIVATE EQUITY: CAREERS, CULTURE, SKILLSETS, AND THE PSYCHOLOGY OF DECISION-MAKING

Private equity is often described through numbers -multiples, returns, IRRs, cash flows, valuations. But those numbers tell only one side of the story. Beneath the surface lies a human world defined by ambition, discipline, pressure, resilience, intuition, and relationships. Private equity is not only a financial industry -it is a profoundly human one. It is built on trust between investors and entrepreneurs, collaboration within teams, judgment under uncertainty, and years of patient engagement with companies, founders, management teams, regulators, and employees. Each investment represents a long-running human relationship, often filled with negotiation, alignment, conflict, compromise, and growth.

This chapter examines private equity not through the lens of financial logic but through the lens of human experience. It explores what it means to build a career in private equity. It dissects the culture of the industry -its work ethic, norms, rituals, and unwritten rules. It analyzes the psychological demands placed on professionals who operate in environments characterized by high stakes, ambiguity, and imperfect information. It explores the role of leadership, emotional intelligence, and interpersonal effectiveness in an industry that is frequently misunderstood as a purely analytical discipline.

While earlier chapters described *how* private equity works, this chapter explores *who* private equity professionals are, what drives them, what challenges them, and what sustains them.

The Allure of Private Equity: Ambition, Influence, and the Craft of Ownership

To understand why people choose careers in private equity, one must begin with its unique appeal. Unlike public market investing, where the investor's role is distant and observational, private equity is deeply immersive. Professionals are not merely buying securities -they are shaping companies. They sit on boards, influence strategy, challenge management teams, negotiate acquisitions, and guide transformations. The work offers the intellectual challenge of investment analysis combined with the tangible impact of business building.

For many, the allure lies in the craft -the idea that private equity is not merely finance but a form of applied problem-solving. Professionals help companies navigate decisions that will define their future: entering new markets, launching new products, rethinking organizational structures, improving supply chains, modernizing technology, optimizing capital allocation, or reimagining customer experiences. Every deal becomes an arena for creativity, discipline, and strategic insight.

Ambition also plays a powerful role. Private equity is a prestigious, high-impact industry. It attracts people who seek challenge, autonomy, influence, and intellectual stimulation. It promises the opportunity to work with extraordinary entrepreneurs, world-class CEOs, and talented peers. It offers compensation that reflects the long-term nature of success, with carry structures that reward performance over years rather than quarters.

But underlying the ambition is a deeper motivation shared by many private equity professionals -the desire to build. Building a company is different from analyzing one. It requires conviction, patience, and resilience. It demands emotional intelligence and operational nuance.

This desire to turn analysis into action is what draws many into the profession and keeps them there despite its demands.

The Culture of Private Equity: A World Defined by Discipline and Intensity

Private equity culture is shaped by a unique combination of rigor, accountability, and long-term orientation. Unlike investment banking, where transactions are the endpoint, private equity views transactions as the beginning of a multi-year journey. The work is measured not in days or weeks but in years -five, seven, sometimes ten years of dialogue, board meetings, strategy sessions, market cycles, and unforeseen challenges.

This long-term horizon fosters a culture of seriousness and responsibility. Professionals must think deeply before making decisions. They must weigh the implications of choices not only for investors but for the hundreds or thousands of employees whose livelihoods depend on the company's success. There is little room for impulsiveness or complacency. Every decision has consequences.

Yet the environment is also intense. Deadlines are real, competitive pressures are strong, and opportunities can vanish quickly if not pursued decisively. Teams operate with high expectations and minimal margin for error. Information is often incomplete, competition is always present, and strategic choices must be made under uncertainty. Excellence is not aspirational -it is required.

The culture is built around dialogue. Investment committee meetings can be intense intellectual arenas where assumptions are challenged, data is dissected, and ideas are tested. Good firms encourage debate; great firms institutionalize it. Junior analysts and associates learn quickly that questions matter as much as answers, and that confidence must be balanced with humility. Senior professionals are judged not only on their decision-making but on their ability to listen, synthesize, and guide.

Over time, this culture shapes the personality of the industry. It fosters resilience, analytical depth, and clarity of thought. But it can also demand stamina, emotional discipline, and a capacity to navigate stress that differs from many other professions.

Career Pathways: From Analyst to Partner, and the Evolution of Responsibility

Careers in private equity are structured yet unpredictable. The industry is hierarchical, but progression is not simply about seniority -it is about developing distinct skills at each stage.

Young analysts begin with analysis -building models, researching markets, reviewing financial statements, and learning the language of investing. They become fluent in valuation, diligence, financial drivers, and strategic frameworks. But their real apprenticeship lies in absorbing how investment professionals think. Analysts learn how senior team members evaluate risk, interpret signals, question assumptions, and synthesize complexity into insight. They learn through observation and iteration.

Associates and senior associates move beyond analysis into decision preparation. They lead diligence workstreams, engage with advisors, meet management teams, and begin forming opinions. Their responsibility expands from answering questions to asking the right ones. They learn that diligence is not about confirming a thesis but about disproving it -or trying to. They become guardians of analytical rigor.

Vice Presidents and Principals transition from execution to leadership. They must originate deals, build relationships with bankers, identify opportunities before competitors see them, and work closely with CEOs and founders. They begin to shape strategy, negotiate terms, structure deals, and manage the subtle interpersonal dynamics of boards and management teams. Their work becomes less about spreadsheets and more about conversations, judgment, and influence.

Partners and Managing Directors carry the burden of ownership. They set the tone for the firm, allocate capital, guide investment themes, and represent the firm to LPs. They navigate complex negotiations, mediate conflicts between founders and investors, make hiring and firing decisions, and shoulder the responsibility for fund performance. Their role is less about technical expertise and more about leadership, trust, and long-term vision.

At each stage, the skills required shift from analytical to relational, from technical to conceptual, from detail-oriented to broad-minded. Private equity careers are rarely linear; they are built on moments of insight, crises navigated, and relationships forged.

The Psychology of Decision-Making: Judgment Under Uncertainty

Private equity investing is fundamentally an exercise in making decisions with incomplete information. Unlike public markets, where data is abundant and price discovery is continuous, private equity operates in opaque environments. Companies often lack perfect data. Markets shift unpredictably. Customer behavior evolves. Competitors adapt. Regulation changes. Macroeconomic conditions shift. Every investment thesis is a hypothesis, not a guarantee.

This uncertainty requires a particular psychological orientation. Investors must embrace ambiguity without being paralyzed by it. They must challenge their own biases -confirmation bias, anchoring, overconfidence, recency bias, narrative fallacy. They must balance optimism with realism, conviction with humility, speed with patience.

Good investors are not those who avoid uncertainty; they are those who navigate it with clarity and discipline. They understand when to rely on data and when to rely on judgment. They recognize that certainty is an illusion and that the goal is not to eliminate risk but to understand its nature.

This psychological resilience is not innate. It is learned through experience -through investments that succeed for unexpected reasons and those that fail despite careful planning. It is learned by watching markets behave irrationally and by observing how companies respond to stress. It is built through years of refining intuition, recognizing patterns, and embracing discomfort.

Interpersonal Dynamics: Founders, CEOs, and the Art of Influence

Private equity is a relationship business. Investors often work with founders who have poured their identity into their companies, with CEOs who must balance strategic ambition with operational reality, and with management teams whose cooperation determines the success of the investment.

Influence, not authority, becomes the core leadership skill. Although private equity investors frequently take board seats, the boardroom provides only limited authority. Most value creation happens through persuasion, collaboration, and credibility. Investors must offer insight without dictating, challenge without alienating, and guide without undermining leadership. They must understand the psychology of founders -ambition, pride, fear, optimism -and navigate it carefully.

In many cases, especially in India, investors work with family-owned businesses. This adds layers of complexity -family dynamics, generational transitions, informal leadership structures, emotional ties, and legacy concerns. Investors must build trust not only with the CEO but with the family, understanding their aspirations and anxieties, aligning incentives, and respecting their identity.

The most successful private equity professionals are those who master empathy. They recognize that companies are not abstract entities -they are human organizations. Understanding those humans becomes central to investment success.

The Emotional Landscape: Pressure, Failure, and Resilience

The private equity profession carries substantial emotional weight. Decisions involve millions or billions of dollars. Responsibilities extend to employees, LPs, founders, and boards. Failures are public, long-lasting, and financially painful. Investments can collapse because of macroeconomic shocks, management missteps, regulatory surprises, or misjudgements in strategy.

Professionals must cope with pressure that is both external and internal. They must maintain composure in front of founders, confidence in front of committees, clarity in front of LPs, and empathy in front of teams. They must navigate stretches of years where investments stagnate, where returns are uncertain, where operational problems mount, and where their own decisions come under scrutiny.

Resilience becomes a defining trait. The ability to withstand surprise. The humility to admit mistakes. The courage to take corrective action. The discipline to follow process even when markets are euphoric. The emotional maturity to separate ego from decision-making.

Behind the polished financial models lies a world of strain, uncertainty, and human complexity.

Leadership in Private Equity: The Evolution of the Modern Investment Leader

Leadership in private equity has evolved dramatically over the past two decades. Early generations of private equity leaders were often financial engineers -masters of leverage, valuation, and structured transactions. Today's leaders must be multi-dimensional. They must be strategists, psychologists, technologists, diplomats, and mentors.

They must build firms capable of lasting beyond their own tenures -ensuring governance, culture, succession planning, and stability. They must nurture talent, build diverse teams, and create environments where discussion is encouraged and dissent is valued. They must navigate LP relationships, manage global teams, and ensure alignment between investment philosophy and organizational behavior.

Great private equity leaders combine clarity of thought with humility of temperament. They know that markets can humble anyone. They know that success is never the result of one individual but of the collective effort of teams, founders, managers, and partners.

The Work-Life Equation: Sustainability and the Redefinition of Success

Private equity has long been known as a demanding profession, one that tests stamina as much as intellect. Long hours, travel, intense deadlines, and periods of high pressure can create imbalance. Yet the industry is gradually shifting. Younger professionals increasingly value holistic success -careers that allow for professional achievement without sacrificing personal fulfillment.

Firms are adapting, slowly but meaningfully. Flexible work rhythms, mental health awareness, structured mentorship, and more deliberate team staffing have become topics of serious attention. The industry has begun to recognize that sustainable performance requires sustainable lifestyles. Burnout does not create strong investors; longevity does.

The new generation of private equity professionals seeks purpose along with prosperity. They want to work on meaningful problems -climate, healthcare, digital access, innovation, education. They value autonomy, learning, and long-term development. They expect humane leadership and inclusive culture.

This generational shift will shape the industry's future as much as macroeconomic or technological trends.

The Ethics and Responsibility of Ownership

Private equity firms control or influence companies that employ millions of people and shape economic outcomes across sectors. With this influence comes responsibility. Ethical decision-making is not a luxury; it is a requirement. Investors must consider the impact of decisions on employees, communities, suppliers, customers, and the environment.

Ethics in private equity extend beyond compliance. They include fair treatment of employees during restructuring, responsible lending practices, sustainable resource use, transparent governance, and adherence to the long-term interests of stakeholders.

The future of private equity will increasingly be judged not only by returns but by stewardship.

Conclusion: The Human Faces Behind the Capital

Private equity is often depicted as a world of capital, contracts, and control. But at its heart, it is a world of humans -driven by ambition, shaped by culture, anchored by values, and defined by decisions made under uncertainty. It is a profession that demands discipline and empathy, intellect and humility, conviction and flexibility.

Behind every investment is a team of individuals striving to understand a business, support a founder, unlock potential, and create long-term value. Behind every return metric is a story of persistence, creativity, and resilience. Behind every firm is a culture -sometimes supportive, sometimes flawed, but always evolving.

Private equity is not just a financial discipline. It is a human discipline. And understanding its human dimension is essential to understanding the industry itself.

CHAPTER 21 -EPILOGUE

Private equity is, at first glance, an industry obsessed with numbers -valuations, multiples, returns, ratios, and models. But when one looks closely, beneath the spreadsheets and structures, one discovers something more fundamental: private equity is a story about belief. Belief in the potential of companies, belief in the ability of teams to transform themselves, belief in the power of disciplined capital to create long-term value, and belief in the promise of the future.

Throughout this book, we have traveled through decades of history, across geographies and industries, through the lives of entrepreneurs, investors, workers, and customers. We have seen private equity evolve from a niche financial craft into a global force shaping economies and societies. We have explored its triumphs and its failures, its innovations and its risks, its complexities and contradictions. And after all this exploration, we return to a simple truth: private equity is ultimately a human endeavor, built on trust, judgment, and stewardship.

The future of private equity -like its past -will not be determined solely by capital abundance or analytical sophistication. It will be defined by how investors choose to use the influence they possess. Will they operate with humility, recognizing that companies are fragile systems built by people with dreams, fears, and aspirations? Will they accept the responsibility that comes with control -the responsibility to create, not merely extract? Will they treat governance not as a box-ticking exercise but as a way of anchoring companies in stability, transparency, and fairness? Will they view sustainability not as a trend but as an obligation to generations that will inherit the outcomes of today's decisions?

Private equity has immense potential to be a force for good -to accelerate innovation, build resilient companies, professionalize leadership, and catalyze growth across sectors and economies. It can help family businesses transition to world-class institutions. It can support entrepreneurs in scaling ideas that change the way people live, work, and connect. It can strengthen industries that form the backbone of nations. It can bring discipline to markets that lack it, and vision to companies that need it.

But private equity also has the capacity to stumble -to chase returns blindly, to overlook governance risks, to prioritize short-term gains over long-term health, to treat companies as financial instruments rather than human organizations. The duality of the industry is real, and acknowledging it is essential.

This book has aimed to portray private equity in its full complexity -not as a hero, not as a villain, but as an evolving discipline. At its best, private equity is a craft practiced with precision and integrity by professionals who understand that capital alone does not build businesses; people do. At its worst, it is a blunt instrument that can destabilize instead of strengthen. The difference lies in choices -choices made in boardrooms, in meetings, in partners' discussions, in diligence processes, and in moments of uncertainty.

This Epilogue is not a conclusion but an invitation -an invitation to approach private equity with both analytical rigor and ethical discernment. To see numbers, but also see people. To evaluate returns, but also evaluate consequences. To understand that ownership is not merely a financial arrangement; it is a responsibility.

The world is entering an era where private capital will influence nearly every aspect of economic and social development. Digital transformation, climate change, healthcare evolution, urbanization, infrastructure demands, demographic shifts -each of these forces will require long-term, patient capital supported by deep expertise. Governments cannot shoulder these transformations alone. Public markets, with their demand for quarterly performance, are often ill-suited to the long-term thinking required. Private equity, with its flexibility, alignment, and strategic capacity, is uniquely positioned to lead.

The next generation of private equity professionals will inherit an industry at a crossroads -richer, more global, more technologically advanced, and more influential than ever before. They will also inherit a world that is more fragile, more interconnected, more uncertain. Their decisions will carry weight not only for their investors, but for societies, economies, and future generations.

If there is a single message that echoes through the pages of this book, it is this: private equity is not simply about creating financial value; it is about creating enduring value. Value that lasts beyond cycles, beyond leadership changes, beyond fund horizons. Value that strengthens companies and communities. Value that reflects wisdom, not just intelligence. Value that embodies stewardship, not just ownership.

As the final chapter closes, the story does not end. Every investment begins a new story. Every partnership opens a new path. Every company backed, every board seat taken, every strategic choice made contributes to the unfolding narrative of private equity -a narrative written not in numbers but in the lives it touches.

May those who enter this industry carry forward both its ambition and its responsibility. May they build companies that endure. May they lead with clarity and integrity. May they remember that behind every decision is a human being who depends on its outcome. And may they leave the industry stronger than they found it.

Private equity is, in the end, a long journey. A journey of capital, yes -but even more, a journey of character.

ENDNOTES & BIBLIOGRAPHY

I. Books & Academic Literature

1. Kaplan, Steven N., and Josh Lerner. *The Future of Private Equity.* Harvard Business School Publishing.
2. Gompers, Paul A., and Josh Lerner. *The Venture Capital Cycle.* MIT Press.
3. Damodaran, Aswath. *Investment Valuation.* Wiley Finance.
4. Damodaran, Aswath. *The Little Book of Valuation.* Wiley.
5. McKinsey & Company. *Valuation: Measuring and Managing the Value of Companies.* Wiley.
6. Phalippou, Ludovic. *Private Equity Laid Bare.* Oxford University Press.
7. Chambers, Andrew, and Glenn Peroni. *Private Equity: History, Governance, and Ethics.*
8. Lowenstein, Roger. *Origins of Financial Markets.*
9. Koller, Tim, Marc Goedhart, and David Wessels. *Valuation: Measuring and Managing the Value of Companies.*
10. Bruner, Robert. *Applied Mergers and Acquisitions.* Wiley.

II. Industry Reports & Research Publications

These are standard references used by professionals across the industry.

1. Bain & Company. *Global Private Equity Report* (Annual Editions).
2. McKinsey & Company. *Global Private Markets Review* (Annual).
3. PitchBook Data. *Private Equity & Venture Capital Market Reports.*
4. Preqin. *Global Alternatives Report.*

5. EY India. *Private Equity and Venture Capital Trends Report.*
6. Grant Thornton India. *Dealtracker Series.*
7. BCG. *Indian Value Creation and Private Capital Landscape Reports.*
8. PwC. *Deals in India* and *PE Insights* series.
9. IMF & World Bank. *Global Economic Prospects.*
10. OECD. *Institutional Investment and Private Markets Reviews.*

III. Regulatory & Legislative Sources

These sources informed the regulatory context for India and global markets.

1. Securities and Exchange Board of India (SEBI). *AIF Regulations.*
2. Reserve Bank of India (RBI). *Foreign Direct Investment Policy Circulars.*
3. Ministry of Finance, Government of India. *Economic Survey* (Annual).
4. Insolvency and Bankruptcy Board of India. *IBC Framework & Quarterly Updates.*
5. Companies Act, 2013 - Ministry of Corporate Affairs, Government of India.
6. US SEC. *Private Fund Adviser Rules & Regulatory Releases.*
7. European Securities and Markets Authority (ESMA). *AIFMD Guidelines.*
8. OECD. *Corporate Governance Principles.*

IV. Case Study & Historical Sources

These include interviews, long-form journalism, and public-domain materials that provided historical or contextual clarity -without directly informing prose.

1. Public filings and investor presentations of Flipkart, Manipal Hospitals, Adani Transmission, Mankind Pharma, Zomato, etc.
2. Business Standard, Economic Times, Mint, and Financial Express archives for public deal information.
3. Reuters Deals, Bloomberg Markets, and CNBC transcripts for historical context on major Indian exits.
4. NASSCOM, IAMAI, CII, and FICCI publications on Indian IT, consumer, and digital sectors.
5. Industry conference papers and public keynote speeches by global GPs and LPs.

V. Quantitative Finance & Valuation Frameworks

1. Modigliani, Franco, and Merton Miller. *Capital Structure Theory.*
2. Sharpe, William F. *Capital Asset Pricing Model (CAPM) Papers.*
3. Jensen, Michael C. *Agency Theory and the Economics of Free Cash Flow.*
4. Black, Fischer, and Myron Scholes. *Option Pricing Theory.*
5. Fama, Eugene, and Kenneth French. *Asset Pricing Factor Models.*
6. Lintner, John. *Corporate Finance Applications.*

VI. Thought Leadership & Practitioner Sources

These materials help contextualize the industry's evolution, without influencing specific text.

1. Harvard Business Review articles on leadership, governance, and organizational behavior.
2. MIT Sloan Management Review: articles on digital transformation, AI, and innovation.
3. Stanford GSB case studies on private equity, buyouts, and venture capital.
4. Wharton Private Equity Review.
5. INSEAD Knowledge: governance and family business insights.
6. Columbia Business School: value investing frameworks applied to private markets.

VII. General References & Macroeconomic Context

1. UN Population Division: demographic projections.
2. World Bank Open Data: macroeconomic datasets.
3. IMF World Economic Outlook.
4. India Brand Equity Foundation (IBEF) sector insights.
5. RBI Handbook of Statistics on the Indian Economy.

Don't miss out!

Visit the website below and you can sign up to receive emails whenever Nishant Prabhakar publishes a new book. There's no charge and no obligation.

https://books2read.com/r/B-A-VCGDF-FRQWI

www.ingramcontent.com/pod-product-compliance
Ingram Content Group UK Ltd.
Pitfield, Milton Keynes, MK11 3LW, UK
UKHW040226290926
15471UKWH00001B/23

9 798224 772582